D1308282

Black Elk Lives

Conversations with the Black Elk Family

By Esther Black Elk DeSersa,
Olivia Black Elk Pourier,
Aaron DeSersa Jr.,
and Clifton DeSersa

EDITED BY HILDA NEIHARDT AND LORI UTECHT
INTRODUCTION BY CHARLES TRIMBLE
University of Nebraska Press
Lincoln and London

⊗

First Nebraska paperback printing: 2003

Library of Congress Cataloging-in-Publication Data

Black Elk DeSersa, Esther.

Black Elk lives: conversations with the Black Elk
family / by Esther Black Elk DeSersa . . . [et al.];
edited by Hilda Neihardt and Lori Utecht;
introduction by Charles Trimble.

p. cm.

Includes bibliographical references and index.

ISBN 0-8032-3340-X (cl.: alk. paper)

ISBN 0-8032-6207-8 (pa.: alk. paper)

1. Black Elk, 1863–1950—Family.   2. Oglala
Indians—Kinship.   3. Oglala Indians—Genealogy.
4. Oglala Indians—Interviews.   5. Black Elk DeSersa, Esther.
I. Petri, Hilda Neihardt.   II. Utecht, Lori.   III. Title.

E99.O3 B532   2000

978.004'9752—dc21

00-028665

Contents

Illustrations

Editors' Preface

This book is in part the result of a chance remark made during a conversation I had a few years ago with Esther Black Elk DeSersa and Olivia Black Elk Pourier. We were discussing certain disturbing statements that had recently been published concerning their grandfather, the famed Lakota holy man. Our mutual concern prompted Esther's question: "Why don't they ask the family?"

Esther's query was so pertinent that we felt it was time to write a new book. In gathering and compiling material for this purpose, we have chosen not to disagree with or refute the disturbing comments referred to above. With our contributors, relatives who lived with and cared for the Lakota holy man, we have chosen to create a book that will provide authentic information about Black Elk, his descendants, and the Lakota people. A visit with the director of the University of Nebraska Press assured us that such a book would be welcome.

When I considered who might be a helpful partner in such an undertaking, Lori Utecht came immediately to mind. Lori is a former director of the John G. Neihardt State Historic Site in Bancroft, Nebraska, has taught at Wayne State College in Wayne, Nebraska, and recently completed her doctoral dissertation on Neihardt's essays at the University of Nebraska.

During the fall and winter of 1995 and 1996, Lori and I drove a number of times to Gordon, Nebraska, where we were joined by Esther, Olivia, Aaron DeSersa, and Clifton DeSersa for day-long talks in our motel rooms. It was understood, of course, that the proposed book should be concerned with their lives on and off the Pine Ridge Reservation and with their memories of Black Elk and his son,

Benjamin (Ben), who did so much to make his father known through-out this country and in Europe. The actual choice of topics, how-ever, was left almost entirely to these family members—Black Elk's caretakers and descendants. It soon became quite clear to Lori and me that the Black Elks had given their book considerable thought, and we found their recollections about themselves and the holy man both refreshing and revealing.

I went again to Gordon in the summer of 1997, accompanied by a writer-friend, Betty Littleton, of Columbia, Missouri, and we camped at Olivia's home near Porcupine, South Dakota.[1] Esther and Clifton joined us, and again our talks were fruitful. Since that time, Esther, Olivia, and Clifton have visited me at my home and at my son's home in Tekamah, Nebraska, and we have continued our communications by telephone and in letters. Aaron has also visited me in recent years.

During our interviews, Lori and I posed questions primarily for the sake of continuity and clarification. We intended to serve only as facilitators for the Black Elks' conversations. Likewise, in the compi-lation and editing of the recorded conversations, we have taken few liberties with the transcripts. Reminiscences about similar subjects given on different days were gathered together in a manner that pre-served the chronology of events, and undue repetition was avoided. Nevertheless, for the most part the memories and comments of the Black Elks appear as they were spoken to us. We have endeavored to preserve each person's manner of expression, although this was not always feasible. For example, the occasional use of the present tense (the Lakota language does not have a past tense, I am told) in referring to past times required change to avoid confusing the reader. During the writing of this book, drafts have been submitted to the Black Elks, who added or deleted material as they wished, and copies of this completed manuscript have been submitted to them for their examination and approval.

During these interviews, Esther once commented that the man-ner of her grandfather's storytelling "had a rhythm to it." In this re-gard, Lori brought my attention to an article that my father, John Neihardt, wrote for the *St. Louis Dispatch* in June 1931, after our return from the Black Elk interviews. Entitled "A Great Indian Poet," Neihardt's article tells of "sitting at the feet of a poet fit to dine with the finest spirits that have sung in this discordant world," and of hearing this seer tell of visions of "astonishing beauty."[2] With these comments, Neihardt opened a public conversation about the Black Elk interviews that continues today.

That public conversation has lately been joined by the voices of those seeking to understand the context in which the book *Black Elk Speaks* was created. The process that took place seemed straightforward enough at the time—Black Elk spoke, his son Ben translated, my sister Enid took notes, and my father edited and shaped the material. With each passing year, however, the relationship between Neihardt and Black Elk has been increasingly clouded by speculation, assumption, and interpretation. Those interested in exploring how the book came to be have asked questions regarding authorship, appropriation, material selection, and other important issues.

But no matter how much today's critics and other readers of *Black Elk Speaks* would like their questions answered, the only two men capable of providing complete answers are no longer living. Thus, we must keep in mind that speculation about motive and methods can be only that—speculation. We can, however, add perspective to the debate and enlarge the picture of what we know. Scholarship of honesty and integrity can enlarge our circle of knowing, as can the inclusion of additional voices to the conversation.

It is in this spirit that Esther Black Elk DeSersa, Olivia Black Elk Pourier, and Lori and I decided to add the voices of Black Elk family members to the conversation. The result is a book rich in memory: the sisters' recollections of witnessing the interviews themselves, remembrances of their grandfather and their father Ben's lifelong efforts to share the story of his father's vision, reflections on their years growing up on the Pine Ridge Reservation, memories of family and tradition. Their voices are joined by those of Aaron and Clifton DeSersa, as they share stories of their lives, and Aaron DeSersa tells of learning from family and tribal elders on his spiritual journey as keeper of the pipe for the family.

But for me this book is more than a collection of trustworthy information that will contribute to a field that is currently of widespread interest: it is a labor of love. Throughout my life I have remembered the meaningful ceremony performed by Black Elk and his friend Standing Bear, a Minneconjou, following the old-time feast held during the 1931 interviews that culminated in the book *Black Elk Speaks*. During that ceremony, my father, my sister Enid, and I were adopted into the Oglala tribe, and each of us was given a personally defining name from Black Elk's great vision. At the end of the ceremony, Black Elk suggested to us something to this effect: "It may happen that in the future you will be in need, and you will turn to us. It may also happen that we shall be in need, and you will help us."

Spoken by a man for whom we had such great respect, those words could not fail to have a great effect on me as an enthusiastic and impressionable fourteen-year-old. Since that memorable event, I have felt somehow related to the Black Elk family, and I have not forgotten the holy man's admonition to us. It is my earnest hope that this book, which contributes both valuable information and affectionate reminiscences from Black Elk's granddaughters and great-grandsons, will not only be of interest and perhaps more than a little historical or scholarly value to readers, but will be of material benefit to the Black Elks.

We are aware that other descendants of Black Elk might have contributed memories that would be worthy of inclusion in a book such as this. It has not been our intention to exclude any such persons, but practical considerations of time and space have made it necessary to concentrate on those with whom we have been in close contact over the years. A family tree, carefully developed by the contributors, will be found in the appendix.

Looking back on our conversations with the holy man's granddaughters and great-grandsons, we can see that our visits brought to each of us a deepening awareness of the meaning of Black Elk's life. This work has made us realize more fully that Black Elk was truly a great man and that his life was a remarkable expression of a fading oral tradition that must somehow be preserved for the benefit of all of us wingless two-leggeds.

And so it is our hope that readers of this book may not only gain a deeper understanding of the lives and present-day thoughts of the Lakota people, but will join the Black Elks in their appreciation of the enduring spiritual contribution made by their grandfather and great-grandfather.

This is their book.

Hilda Neihardt
Lori Utecht

Introduction

This is the story told by the granddaughters of the Lakota holy man Black Elk. Esther DeSersa and Olivia Pourier are the daughters of Benjamin Black Elk, the third child of Nicholas, which was the old holy man's Christian name.

Benjamin, or Ben, as he preferred to be called, was born on the Pine Ridge Reservation in 1899 and died in 1973. He was a respected tribal historian, politician, and advisor, and took seriously his self-appointed role as ambassador-at-large for Lakota people. In great demand as a speaker, he talked to high school and college convocations as well as civic organizations throughout the West.

Following in the footsteps of his father (who often performed at tourist centers in the Black Hills throughout the 1930s and 1940s), Ben spent most summers after World War II at the Mount Rushmore National Monument, posing in traditional regalia for tourist photographers and telling stories—based on Lakota legend—to their children. Postcards of him in various poses with the granite faces in the background have sold in the millions over the years in gift shops throughout the West, earning him the sobriquet "the fifth face on Rushmore."

When he was yet a child, Ben attended Carlisle Indian School in Pennsylvania for a short time. Returning to the reservation, he finished his schooling at Holy Rosary Mission, a Jesuit-run boarding school near the village of Pine Ridge. The mission school, in those early years, went only to the eighth grade, and that was the extent of Ben's formal education.

Through much of the twentieth century, religion on the Pine Ridge Reservation—or the religion practiced openly—was Christian, mostly Roman Catholic and Episcopalian. Although forbidden by federal policy, traditional religious practices, especially *yuwípi,* continued in more remote areas, and generally in secret.[1]

To the well-meaning "reformers" who held great influence over the formation of Indian policy following the Civil War, "civilizing" the Indians demanded that they be brought into Christianity and that their pagan beliefs and practices be destroyed. Thus Christianity became the state religion as it applied to the tribes, and zero-tolerance became official policy as it applied to Native religions.

Pursuant to this policy, newly established reservations, to which the various tribes were confined in the latter part of the nineteenth century, were assigned to different Christian denominations, which then had exclusive rights to proselytize. This, obviously, was to preclude competition and bickering among the denominations on any reservation. The Catholic Church, as early as the mid–eighteenth century, had made strong inroads into Sioux country by virtue of the predominance of the church among the earliest trappers and traders, mostly French, who ventured into that territory. So, although the Pine Ridge reservation was assigned to the Episcopal Church, the Catholic Church already had a foothold there, which grew in strength with the conversion of Chief Red Cloud by the Jesuits.

The older Black Elk, Nicholas, converted to Catholicism in 1904 and was made a catechist. Catechists were respected tribal elders who, because of the dearth of priests to cover the far-flung reaches of the reservations, were recruited to serve certain pastoral functions in the parishes, including prayer services on Sabbath and holy days.

In recent times, with the belated popularity of John Neihardt's book *Black Elk Speaks,* considerable controversy has arisen, mainly in academic and philosophical circles, over the holy man's seemingly dichotomous religious holdings. Some argue that, given his stature and the power of his visions, Black Elk could not have been a true believer in the Catholic faith. Others argue that his service as a purveyor among his people of Roman Catholic doctrine had tainted him and rendered his words, as told to Neihardt, unworthy of the great respect that they carry among younger generations of his own people and non-Indian followers alike.

In *Black Elk Speaks,* Black Elk concludes his great story with words of deep sorrow over having failed the mission of his sacred vision as a Lakota holy man: "And I, to whom a great vision was given in my youth—you see me now a pitiful old man who has done nothing, for the nation's hoop is broken and scattered. There is no center any longer, and the sacred tree is dead."[2] To Neihardt's question as to his conversion to Catholicism the old man responded only, "My children have to live in this world." Neihardt probed no further.

Nevertheless, he lived out his life as a Catholic and was buried in a Catholic cemetery with full rites of the church. He raised his children in the faith, and his granddaughters are Catholics. According to Jesuit writer Paul Manhart (in an interview with Edward Trandahl appearing in the *Omaha World Herald,* 8 November 1975), "Black Elk fitted the cultures together like a puzzle and thus neither was dissolved."

The controversy that goes on in academic and literary circles has had little if any effect on the reputation of the holy man or his descendants in either the traditional or Christian communities on the reservation today. *Black Elk Speaks* remains an important document in the preservation and practice of Lakota belief and ritual, and the Black Elk family holds a respected place in Lakota society.

To better understand the Black Elk family's story, it is important to know something about the environment in which they live on the Pine Ridge Indian Reservation. The Pine Ridge Indian Reservation is the homeland of the Oglala Lakota, or Sioux, which is the largest and westernmost of seven tribes that make up the Teton Lakota Nation.[3] Located in southwestern South Dakota, the reservation spans over five thousand square miles of arid grasslands, veined with creek valleys studded with groves of cottonwood. On the southern edge are rolling hills with stands of ponderosa pine, hence the name Pine Ridge. On the northern tier are vast expanses of stark lunar landscapes of the Badlands, a final stronghold in the tragic last days of the Sioux's ghost dance resistance.

The reservation population today is estimated at slightly under twenty thousand, with a majority of the Oglalas living in or within several miles around Pine Ridge Village, the seat of tribal government and headquarters of the various federal agencies serving the tribe. The remainder of the tribal population lives in small communities scattered throughout the reservation, most of which were established in the early reservation days around traditional bands made up of extended families, called *thiyóšpaye* in the Lakota language. Whites number slightly more than 1,500, mostly employees of the federal agencies, medical employees in the federal hospital, teachers in tribal schools, and ranchers who lease Indian lands.

There has been little economic growth of any significant scale on the reservation since before World War II. Up to that time, Indians in the isolated communities there sustained themselves with some small business activity and small-scale agriculture, mostly cattle ranching and subsistence gardening. Now, according to the Department of Commerce, the reservation encompasses the single poorest county in the United States.[4]

Life on the reservation is characterized by social pathology, manifested in rampant alcoholism, family disintegration, an alarming rate of suicide among teenagers, a violent crime rate out of all proportion to the rest of rural America—much of it tied to alcohol—and increasing youth gang activity. Health conditions are poor, with a high incidence of malnutrition, diabetes, and even tuberculosis. Such chronic conditions are attributed largely to pervasive dependency fostered by decades of colonial control over life and tribal resources by a paternalistic federal bureaucracy in its role as trustee.

Considering this sad state, one wonders if holy man Black Elk's lament, "the nation's hoop is broken and scattered . . . the sacred tree is dead," might not have been prophecy.

But this land of the Oglala is not, as fund-raising letters for reservation schools and clinics often describe it, "a land of despair," for such describes a people without hope, a defeated people. The Oglala Sioux are a strong, resilient people with faith in their culture and hope for the future of their homelands. This faith and hope is exemplified by the fact that their poverty-ridden tribe has since 1980, when the Sioux tribes were awarded more than $100 million in compensation for the illegal taking of the Black Hills by the U.S. government, consistently declined to accept any of that money for fear of jeopardizing even the faintest possibility of restoration to them of some of their sacred Pahá Sápa lands. The other Sioux tribes named as beneficiaries to the settlement have followed suit and have also declined to accept their shares.

There is a strong resurgence of traditional Lakota belief among the Oglalas—in religious practices, medicine, pageantry, and school studies. Pride in traditional Lakota culture is now seen by tribal service programs as a means of addressing social problems and is incorporated into counseling on alcoholism, drug abuse, and other areas. Christian churches on the reservation are adopting Lakota designs in their décor and vestments, and incorporating into their own ceremonies such rituals as blessing with the smoke of sweet grass.

After his pathetic lament, old Black Elk added, "But if the vision was true and mighty, as I know, it is true and mighty yet; for such things are of the spirit." [5]

The Black Elk granddaughters, Esther and Olivia, and their families live in the Wounded Knee district, the most scenic area of the reservation. It was here that John Neihardt in 1930 was directed to find what he was searching for—a Sioux medicine man, who might give insight into the Messiah movement that led to the Wounded Knee tragedy. Instead he found a holy man, whose story would place both their names in homes and libraries throughout the world. The families live in conditions that in most of white America might be seen as poverty. Their homes and villages lack much of the comforts, even necessities, which are found even in the most devastated inner cities. Abundant in their homes instead is great faith, patience, love, and happiness. There is warm friendship for neighbors as well as strangers, humor that is catching, and that most important Lakota value, generosity. These all come forth in their story.

Charles Trimble

Part 1. The Black Elk Family

The Legacy

by Benjamin Black Elk

Chosen by his father to interpret what he told Neihardt in the 1931 interviews (which later were incorporated into the book Black Elk Speaks*), Ben Black Elk became something of a disciple of his father. Ben traveled widely in this country and in Europe, telling about the Lakota holy man and about his people and their religion. Ben was the father and grandfather of the contributors to this book, and his life and experiences are of considerable importance in the Black Elk story. His children and grandchildren have much to tell about Ben; but we begin with a talk which he, with help from his son Henry, gave in 1969 at Pine Ridge Boarding School, Pine Ridge, South Dakota, at the request of Warfield Moose Sr., a teacher at that institution. Esther has a recording of that talk, and Olivia provided a transcription, which has been edited for clarity and readability.*

Well, I am Black Elk, Ben, the son of the famous Indian you read so much about in *Black Elk Speaks,* and I've come a long way. I have learned quite a bit by experience, and I shall start my life history way back from what I learned about our Indians, the Sioux, especially the Oglala Sioux.

I was born in the year 1899, May the seventeenth, so in a few days—Saturday—I'll be seventy years old. My mind goes back, way back, to when my grandmother and grandfather really fought Custer, and there were really Indians at that time. Eighteen ninety-nine is just a few years after the establishment of this reservation, Pine Ridge, and I can still remember that at that time some of those Indians had two wives. My grandfather, Black Elk, my father's father, was wounded at Fetterman's Fight. We called that The Year of the Hundred Soldiers Slain.

So my grandmother became a widow, and she had a first cousin, who married the famous Indian that we read so much about—Good Thunder—who was an instigator of the ghost dance.[1]

I lost my mother when I was about a year old, so I had to live here and there with my grandmother on my mother's side, then also with the grandmother on my father's side. I always remember when my grandfather, Good Thunder, died; he had a heart attack. I must have been about five years old, and at that time the Indians mourned, they really mourned, for their loved ones. So when the loved one died, they really went—well, we'll say, probably not haywire—but they grieved. They cut themselves on the leg. So my two grandmothers—Good Thunder had two wives, one was my own grandmother and the other was our first cousin—built up a big tipi and laid him in there, and my grandmothers went around and cried, wailing for their husband that had passed away. I must have been about four or five years old, but I remember that.

Later, I was raised by my grandmothers, either my father's mother or my mother's mother, and soon I went to school. And at that time I had full braids; I had long hair down to below my belt. So when I went to school, I had an aunt that raised me at that time and at the give-away. They helped the needy at that time. Anybody today who possesses a lot of money and a mansion, he's probably somebody, but to us Indians, it's not good. It doesn't do any good, because he hasn't helped other Indians. At that time, when I was a boy, the Indians really helped each other. So when I went to school the first time, they cut my four braids off, and it cost my aunt four horses: for each braid they cut, she gave a horse to an Indian.

At the age of thirteen I went to Carlisle, Pennsylvania; there I lived among the white people for almost five years. I worked for the people, stayed out on the farm, and I became interested in my people. I took up Indian culture, so when I came home, I got married and settled down in this place, this very place I'm talking from. From right here you can see the white buttes out there, the beautiful scenery, and I feel like this is Crazy Horse land, because Crazy Horse is buried someplace around here. Every morning I go out and I see those white bluffs, and they are nature's monuments to Crazy Horse. I learned from my elders, such as my father, who was the best teacher I ever had. He was a medicine man, and I mention also Frank Good Lance—all those old people.

I learned about the pipe and the ways of our culture; it is good. But I feel today that that has gone. We have come a long way, lived through the centuries up until now, these modern times—the atomic age—guided by the Great Spirit. But today is so different that we like to go back and dream about our own people.

My father was quite a man. John Neihardt came to write the story of Crazy Horse, but when he had stayed a month, he found out that my father was quite a character, so he wrote the book *Black Elk Speaks.*[2] Later another man came and wrote *The Sacred Pipe.*[3]

I have led two lives—one as a Christian and one as a believer of the Indian religion. So when I lecture on Indian religion, I feel that I am trying to tear down Christianity, but that isn't so. Today it has all merged together, and I feel that I live the one life now, which is our modern religion.

Let's talk about, maybe, five hundred years ago, when this whole country was a paradise. We Indians didn't know what a dollar was, what whiskey was, what coffee was, but we got along. We ate the things that Mother Nature provided for us, especially the buffalo. We got our home, whatever we wore, our moccasins—all were made from the buffalo. And those were the good old days. Seems like the Indian at that time lived a religious life, and they prayed constantly all the time.

At this time, I'd like to talk about the word *wašíchu.* In Indian, that word was used a long time ago. When they are moving out, the scout is sent, and then the scout returns. So he points, takes his big finger and touches the ground and he swears by Mother Earth that what he says he saw is no lie, but the straight truth. Then he says, "I went to the first ridge, I saw buffalo . . . Next ridge, I saw another herd; the third ridge, many buffalo; but the fourth ridge I went to, the buffalo were *wašíchu.*" It means so many buffalo at one time that they cannot get rid of them. So *wašíchu* means so many that you could never get rid of them. Today it stands proved that you can never get rid of the white man: they come, they flow down this country just like water. They are a part of us now. Today we have around about forty-five thousand Sioux in South Dakota, and about 85 percent are mixed-blood, and there are only about 15 percent full-blood.

On this reservation, we have lots to see. Pine Ridge has more potential for tourism than any other reservation, I think, because we have Red Cloud and we have Crazy Horse buried here. Today what the tourist wants to see, number one, is Indians. Number two is cowboys. You might think that Mount Rushmore comes first, but it comes third. I've been up there about twenty-two years. So if you tourists are eager to see our country over here, our Sioux Reservation, you can come down through Scenic Highway 40, and then you can take another highway that turns toward the south, through the Badlands. And when you get through, why, it's beautiful scenery, and you'll find out that the Badlands, so-called by the Indians, used to be no good, nothing grew on it, only rattlesnakes. There is no place in the world like these Badlands, and it's really become valuable to our state and also to our tribe here.

Then you can come down through Rocky Ford, and there is a fork in the road, but you take the right one that tells you it's nineteen miles to Manderson, then you come to our park over here. We have a park called Crazy Horse Park, a new one. And you can stop there; we have a camping ground there, and you can camp there for two or three days and even ride around and talk to us, find out how we live and learn firsthand about our Indians. Then you can come—and, by the way, my father's buried there at the cemetery. Then you can go to Wounded Knee; that's where we had our last skirmish with the army. Then you can probably go to Pine Ridge—for the Pine Ridge Oglala Sioux here, our tribal government. You can go through our schools; you are welcome to do so.

Now, as I say, Red Cloud had in mind that we had to give up, and he wanted us to be educated, and he established that school. So there is a song to him. When you translate it, it means a lot to me. And all those that know the song, they realize that what he said is true, especially today, when our culture is so taken away from us by the white man, and they're trying to get their culture down our throats.

The words of the song go like this: "Red Cloud, he told me to be the white man; difficulties I have, but he told me to be the white man; difficulties I have; they are talking about me."

See what we mean, difficulty, we just want to go on, but we can't. We've got to get education, our only salvation; we have to educate our children. Right now, in Washington DC and all over the country, they're confused about our culture. We try to have a comeback for our culture, so that the Indian can identify himself as an Indian in order to get along in this world, to be proud to be an Indian. We have known a lot of Indians that are not proud, that even are ashamed that they're Indians. And I can say that Indian culture is so great, that there is no other, I think, to compete with us.

What I mean is, at one time, we knew what respect was. At one time, if your tongue was forked, why you could not be an Indian, a good Indian. But our whites, white people who taught us the culture of the white man, made us all forked-tongue. So that's what we're trying to do, to get back on the basis where we realize we are Indians.

I started to school when I was seven years old. I couldn't speak a word of English. I had long hair down to my waist and tied in four braids. When I made progress in school, a braid was cut off to mark my progress. Each time my braid was cut off, my aunt would give away a horse to some needy person. They would do this because it was an honor to be in school. Now this shows a big difference in Indian culture. The white man's culture, you see—when the white man's boy makes progress in school, the boy gets a gift, but the Indian way is to mark the progress by making a gift to some needy person. From the time an Indian child is able to understand, he hears about the good of being generous.

In my day, the Indian boy started life differently than today. In those days, sons belonged to Dad; he had to train them. At six months the dad starts holding the baby in the water and lets him get used to the water. Then by the time he is two years old, that little fellow can swim. I learned to ride a horse when I was four years old; later I played games that were taught to make a boy a warrior. One game was called "willows in mud." We took off our shirts; we would take willows and mud and throw them at each other and switch each other, but just on the body. If you hit somebody in the face, you lost a point. This trained us in the joints, because it really stings. And another game was to take the core from a sunflower stock. We would put it on our arms and light it, and you were not supposed to flinch. The other boys wanted to see you flinch. Sometimes I wonder if this isn't why so many of our people can endure so much poverty and suffering without crying or begging or making demonstrations.

When I was born, the massacre at Wounded Knee had happened just nine years before.[4] My father was wounded in that battle. It was the last battle between the Indians and the army.

The massacre at Wounded Knee was the result of an Indian prayer. You have heard of the ghost dance; it was a prayer that was danced. The Indians were desperate; all they had, the great buffalo herds, were all gone. Then someone came along and told the Indians: "I am the Messiah; I am Christ."[5] He said the white man had sinned against him, and if we will do the ghost dance, the white man will disappear and the buffalo and the old ways would come back. We were to throw all our weapons away. We just had to dance and sing this ghost dance song. They thought it would come, but it never came. Instead, we had the massacre at Wounded Knee, and they killed the men, women, and children. The sadness—the sadness of this is still in our hearts.

In his book *Black Elk Speaks* my father said: "When I look back now from this high hill of my old age, I can still see the butchered women and children lying heaped and scattered all along the crooked gulch as plain as when I saw them with eyes still young. . . . A people's dream died there. It was a beautiful dream."[6]

In the old days, the Indian taught that we must love each other. Our belief is that this love was established here on earth by the Great Spirit. This brought us unity; unity brought us brotherhood. We didn't know what a dollar was, but we knew that there was a God, and we kept this sacred. My father said: "This is sacred. Keep it such." We became Christians. We wanted to keep some of our old ceremonies. When we pray, we don't read from a book. It comes from our hearts. But the government outlawed some of our worship, like the sun dance, so we had to do our ceremonies secretly—where we would not be caught. That made us feel bad. It was like the early Christians who had to worship secretly.

So I used to lead two lives: one, Indian religion, and one as a Christian. To us, the Indian pipe is sacred; it has meaning for us. It used to be that when I would speak about the pipe, when I used the pipe, it seemed to me that it clashed with Christianity. But now, I know they come together in our church. Behind the altar, we have the tipi design. In our Christian ceremonials, we use the pipe. We see there is no clash. After these years it comes together. Now, I live only one way. I can be free in what I tell and what I do. That is the way of it, and this is the way it should be in education for all Indian children. I told them in Washington, if they would do like they do here at Red Cloud Indian School, there would not be so many dropouts and so many failures. In the courses that have been created here, the boys and girls learn through the true history of the people.

They teach about the great Indian leaders as well as the great Americans like George Washington and Abraham Lincoln; this gives the true history of the country. They can see themselves as part of the history. I told them that our children here are taught the difference between the white man's ways and the Indian ways—how the Indian ways fit into the white man's world. So when Senator Kennedy came to Pine Ridge, he took time out to come to Red Cloud School and see for himself what he had heard from me and others at the Wounded Knee hearings meeting, where those who testified said the same thing.

In the olden days the Indian was taught to be a man, to have self-respect, to use his initiative. Now, for many years, people have been teaching the Indians that the white way is superior, that the Indian ways are no good. There are many good things in the white man's culture we should use, but the best part of our Indian culture should be retained, taught in our schools as they grow up. Be proud to be an Indian. This is how I feel about teaching our children here at Red Cloud School. We Indians, in a different way, can make the beautiful dream come true. Besides, the people's broken hoop—that could be pulled together.

All right, at this time, I'd like to sing an honor song to our tribal president Enos Poor Bear. You know, he's taken the place of Red Cloud, Crazy Horse, Sitting Bull, and Spotted Tail and other chiefs, and he's trying to lead the people out of what is causing our turmoil. So here we go with our honor song for Enos Poor Bear. [Sings]

HENRY BLACK ELK: Well folks, so much for Red Cloud. Now we'll take you back to Wounded Knee, where the tragedy happened years ago and we'll tell you how it happened and my father will tell you about it. This is taken from *Black Elk Speaks.* So here we go with how it happened:

It was now near the end of the Moon of Popping Trees, and I was twenty-seven years old (December, 1890). We heard that Big Foot was coming down from the Badlands with nearly four hundred people. Some of these were from Sitting Bull's band. They had run away when Sitting Bull was killed and joined Big Foot on Good River. There were only about a hundred warriors in this band, and all the others were women and children and some old men. They were all starving and freezing, and Big Foot was so sick that they had to bring him along on a pony drag. They had all run away to hide in the Badlands, and they were coming in now because they were starving and freezing. When they crossed Smoky Earth River, they followed up Medicine Root Creek to its head. Soldiers were over there looking for them. The soldiers had everything and were not freezing and starving. Near Porcupine Butte the soldiers came up to the Big Foots, and they surrendered and went along with the soldiers to Wounded Knee Creek where the Brenan store is now.

It was in the evening when we heard that the Big Foots were camped over there with the soldiers, about fifteen miles by the old road from where we were. It was the next morning (December 29, 1890) that something terrible happened. . . . [253–54]

In a little while we had come to the top of the ridge where, looking to the east, you can see for the first time the monument and the burying ground on the little hill where the church is. That is where the terrible thing started. Just south of the bury-

ing ground on the little hill a deep dry gulch runs about east and
west, very crooked, and it rises westward to nearly the top of the
ridge where we were. It had no name, but the Wasichus [*wašícus*]
sometimes call it Battle Creek now. We stopped on the ridge not
far from the head of the dry gulch. Wagon guns were still going
off over there on the little hill, and they were going off again
where they hit along the gulch. There was much shooting down
yonder and there were many cries, and we could see cavalrymen scattered over the hills ahead of us. Cavalrymen were riding
along the gulch and shooting into it, where the women and children were running away and trying to hide in the gullies and the
stunted pines.

A little way ahead of us, just below the head of the dry gulch,
there were some women and children who had huddled under a
clay bank, and some cavalrymen were pointing guns at them. . . .
[257]

By now many other Lakotas, who had heard the shooting, were
coming up from Pine Ridge, and we all charged on the soldiers.
They ran eastward toward where the trouble began. We followed
down along the dry gulch, and what we saw was terrible. Dead
and wounded women and children and little babies were scattered all along there where they had been trying to run away.
The soldiers had followed them along the gulch, as they ran, and
murdered them in there. Sometimes they were in heaps because
they had huddled together, and some were scattered all along.
Sometimes bunches of them had been killed and torn to pieces
where the wagon guns hit them. I saw a baby trying to suck its
mother, but she was bloody and dead.

There were two little boys at one place in the gulch. They had
guns and they had been killing soldiers all by themselves. We
could see the soldiers they had killed. The boys were all alone
there, and they were not hurt. These were very brave little boys.

When we drove the soldiers back, they dug themselves in, and
we were not enough people to drive them out from there. In the
evening they marched off up Wounded Knee Creek, and then we
saw all that they had done there.

Men and women and children were heaped and scattered all over the flat at the bottom of the little hill where the soldiers had their wagon-guns, and westward up the dry gulch all the way to the high ridge, the dead women and children and babies were scattered.

When I saw this I wished that I had died too, but I was not sorry for the women and children. It was better for them to be happy in the other world, and I wanted to be there too. But before I went there I wanted to have revenge. I thought there might be a day, and we should have revenge.

After the soldiers marched away, I heard from my friend Dog Chief how the trouble started, and he was right there by Yellow Bird when it happened. This is the way it was:

In the morning the soldiers began to take all the guns away from the Big Foots, who were camped in the flat below the little hill where the monument and burying ground are now. The people had stacked most of their guns, and even their knives, by the tepee where Big Foot was lying sick. Soldiers were on the little hill and all around, and there were soldiers across the dry gulch to the south and over east along Wounded Knee Creek too. The people were nearly surrounded, and the wagon-guns were pointing at them.

Some had not yet given up their guns, and so the soldiers were searching all the tepees, throwing things around and poking into everything. There was a man called Yellow Bird, and he and another man were standing in front of the tepee where Big Foot was lying sick. They had white sheets around and over them, with eyeholes to look through, and they had guns under these. An officer came to search them. He took the other man's gun, and then started to take Yellow Bird's. But Yellow Bird would not let go. He wrestled with the officer, and while they were wrestling, the gun went off and killed the officer. Wasichus [*wašícus*]and some others have said he meant to do this, but Dog Chief was standing right there, and he told me it was not so. As soon as the gun went off, Dog Chief told me, an officer shot and killed Big Foot, who was lying sick inside the tepee.

Then suddenly nobody knew what was happening, except that the soldiers were all shooting and the wagon-guns were going off right in among the people.

Many were shot down right there. The women and children ran into the gulch and up west, dropping all the time, for the soldiers shot them as they ran. There were only about a hundred warriors and there were nearly five hundred soldiers. The warriors rushed to where they had piled their guns and knives. They fought soldiers with only their hands until they got their guns.

Dog Chief saw Yellow Bird run into a tepee with his gun, and from there he killed soldiers until the tepee caught fire. Then he died full of bullets.

It was a good winter day when all this happened. The sun was shining. But after the soldiers marched away from their dirty work, a heavy snow began to fall. The wind came up in the night. There was a big blizzard, and it grew very cold. The snow drifted deep in the crooked gulch, and it was one long grave of butchered women and children and babies, who had never done any harm and were only trying to run away. . . . [259-62]

And so it was all over.

I did not know then how much was ended. When I look back now from this high hill of my old age, I can still see the butchered women and children lying heaped and scattered all along the crooked gulch as plain as when I saw them with eyes still young. And I can see that something else died there in the bloody mud, and was buried in the blizzard. A people's dream died there. It was a beautiful dream.

And I, [Black Elk] to whom so great a vision was given in my youth,—you see me now a pitiful old man who has done nothing, for the nation's hoop is broken and scattered. There is no center any longer, and the sacred tree is dead. [270]

BEN BLACK ELK: The narrator was Henry Black Elk, my son, and I am doing the background, the chanting background—the songs, the songs of the ghost dance. This has been taken from *Black Elk Speaks* and *The Song of the Messiah* by John Neihardt.[7]

HENRY BLACK ELK:

A gunshot ripped the hush. The panic roar
Outfled the clamor of the hills and died.
And then—as though the whole world, crucified
Upon the heaped Golgotha of its years,
For all its lonely silences of tears,
Its countless hates and hurts and terrors, found
A last composite voice—a hell of sound
Assailed the brooding heavens. Once again
The wild wind-roaring of the rage of men,
The blent staccato thunders of the dream,
The long-drawn, unresolving nightmare scream
Of women and of children over all!
Now—now at last—the peace of love would fall,
And in a sudden stillness, very kind
The blind would look astonished on the blind
To lose their little dreams of fear and wrath!

BEN BLACK ELK: How, Kola! Ah, I kind of like this. I love it, you know. It's just like when I'm in the movies and they introduce me. They say, "Oh, Black Elk is in the movies," and all this and that. They praise me up like that, but there is one thing they always forget. And it's a matter of record, and you may jot it down, but I been here first and I'm still here! But anyway, I'd like to talk to you about the Indian religion. I have long studied my people. I'm a full-blood Indian; I have no master's degree or no education. I just picked it up, and I've studied my people. I lived it. I sing the songs. I know these two books, *Black Elk Speaks,* that's my father's book, and *The Sacred Pipe,* so I'm pretty well informed, maybe. I would like to tell this in common English, not in a technical way, because I couldn't do it, but I'll try to put it all like this.

You know, I acted in a picture one time.[8] I came out of the brush on horseback, and the horse reared up, and there were a lot of tipis down there, and I said like this: "This is the Black Hills. I am Black Elk. This is the home of my people, the Lakotas, with the sky our father and the earth our mother; we have come a long, long way, and we have lived through the centuries, guided by the Great Spirit. Our history has been written on the four winds, only to be captured by our wise men, which is handed down generation to generation, our own kin files, so that's the way we lived at one time. Today, we put it in books, but I'm sure you like to hear from somebody that lived it. And I'm sure that as we go along, we learn a lot about the Indian; the Indian religion was so great."

We didn't know where we'd come from, and that's a question I have always tried to answer. I get all my studies—all of my experience—I talk to the old-timers, the medicine men. Such men as my father, such men as Little Warrior—you've heard of him. Such men as Good Lance, and such men as Chips. I was just a youngster, but I wanted to know.

So I took up the drum, and whenever they performed a ceremonial, I joined it. And the way I understand it, they say we are survivors of destruction. Geologists tell us these old Black Hills are the oldest mountains in the world. They been here, being pushed up by earthquakes, so it came up. And then they claimed the Indian believed that that is the center of the universe; it's so sacred to them they go there to lament or to hunt. The Indian believes he lives in a cycle, and this old world, they claim, has been destroyed and overhauled. In other words, you have a car, it don't run good, you put in pistons, and maybe it run like a top again.

So that's the way the Indians believe. We knew there is a god. And they claim, according to my father's book, and other Indians, that this is our last stage—what we call the fire age. And the Bible tells us we're going to destroy ourselves by fire, and that is putting it close at hand.

So, all in all, what the Indian tells us—they claim we are survivors of destruction. We cannot prove we came by the Bering Strait. Maybe we came by boat, and we Sioux, we claim that we are the originals that ever came here. Because other tribes belong to us, and at one time they dispersed, so we say, in the seven camps. At one time they got along fine, and then they couldn't get along, so they decided they must disperse, and they claim that's the way your other tribes came in, so we don't talk like we used to; our language differs as we go along. To prove that—the Osages, we've never contacted them as long as I remember, as long as the old-timers told me, they never contacted them, but they talk like we do. I had contacted one Osage up at Mount Rushmore, and I talked to him in Sioux language, and I understood him, and he understood me.

The Indian believes in prayer that comes from the heart—the heart alone. They meditate along the creek, and the creek will talk to you; you will find out the truth there. Who is the supreme power? Why do the little birds fly? And little grasses come up? There is only one prayer the Indian uses: "Oh, Great Spirit, be merciful to me, that my people may live."

When we say "my people" in the Sioux, we say *oyáte. Oyáte* means the whole universe that God created. The little ants are people—they give us an example; the elk are people; the buffalo are people—we learn from them. And the trees, everything that God the Great Spirit created points up to the heavens; it's one. That's why we have the tipi. We have a tipi where we tie a lot of poles; each one stands for something. There is one pole that stands for the Great Spirit in every tipi, in your heart. So the Indians were the greatest religious people on the face of the earth. Everything they say, it's a prayer to the Great Spirit. We send our voices through the rocks, through the trees; after all, they're people. We send our voices, just like the Catholics. They pray to the saints; we do, too, through the rocks.

Now let's talk about the rock; after all, that rock, I am a part of that rock. And all that comes all in one. We'll say that they believe that the Great Spirit has established four, five, six spirits that my father tells about in his book. We say the west—the color of the west is black, because, right now, we're just dying for rain, and that rain feels pretty good! That's where the sun goes down. White is the north. The north is where the White Giant lives—Waziyata. We get our strength and our health and our purity from the north; that spirit helps us. Then let's go to the east; the east is red. By the way—black—I'll come back to black, because the white man mourns in black, but we rejoice with black, so when we wiped out Custer, we blacked our faces and then we danced for joy.

East is red. Red is a danger signal for the whites, but that is our knowledge. We get knowledge from the east because of the light of day. The Indian does the creation of the universe just like the Catholics do, the sacrificial mass, that Christ has come down and died for us again, every day. Well, the Indian, he built his tipi to the east, and he does the creation of the universe. Let's try that tonight. Tonight, let's put all the lights out—the whole lights, put them out—now you don't know where you are. The east reminds us that there is no death, because of the dawn of the day, it is a vision of the life and the death, but that's where we get our knowledge. We have to get up early and meet the sun's light. God said, "Let there be light."

Then later, when the light comes, you can hear the cows mooing, the horses neighing, the dogs barking. Pretty soon the birds are singing. And the creation of the universe happens every morning, but we never realize it. Then the light comes, and that's the light of the eternal light from the Great Spirit. It will never end, never end. One way, one way. That's why the Indian lives one way. His people are in a circle; the circle is what we call the Nation's Hoop, and in the middle of it there is the tree of life, that had bloomed one time.

My father started his prayer—that tree is with it. This is a paradise; we had elk, deer, everything. We didn't know what whiskey was; we didn't know what money was. Our downfall was when the white man came. But here now, this old world is cruel, a cruel world, but we have to adjust ourselves according to modern times, and that is what we are trying to do. So we get our smartness from the east. Later on, when the Indian laments on the hills, he gets his vision, he gets his knowledge.

Then let's go to the south. South is the source of life. Every female in this world represents Mother Earth. Even trees, we have male trees, female trees here. So all females represent Mother Earth. So when you get in the other class, we'll tell you about the women folks. So yellow is south. That's why when a man, a warrior, goes out on the warpath he paints his face yellow. I have that symbol, you know. Twenty years ago—twenty-two, twenty-three years ago—when I started out at Mount Rushmore, I became a showman. My father was alive, so I couldn't be a chief, so I posed as the only Indian who is not a chief, and it stuck! Today, I am still the only Indian that is not a chief! So I stuck to that yellow—yellow markings. Some day I'll be a chief. There's a story to that.

I been up at Mount Rushmore for twenty-two years and all the bus drivers getting the tourists out there, they know my life, and they know my biography. So the driver tells them there is a chief out there, and in the evening you can have a picture with him. And one tourist said, "I know Black Elk. I come there almost every year; I have a picture of him, and I notice that he's not a chief, yet he wears one feather. And I wonder why he is not a chief."

So he told me, "I know that story. Ben Black Elk has a brother. His name is Falling Rocks. So Black Elk and his brother were two good guys; they were two good brothers, and they could shoot anything, and they were fit to be chiefs. So when old man Black Elk was dying, he gave a certain amount of arrows to go out and the one who brought the most game would be the chief. So Black Elk—Ben—he came back with the game, but his brother never came back. And they never found him yet—never did come back. So, at this time, all the highway departments all over the nation, they're looking for Falling Rocks. They got signs up there on the road: "Look out for falling rocks."

But that's how I came back. Anyway, let's go back to the four cardinals. Green is earth—green. And the color blue is heaven. Now the Indians say "Até Wakhą́ Tháka"—they say "father." And then again they say "Tunkashila" [Thųkášila]—"grandfather." Our pipe is older than Christianity. Our religion, our Indian religion, is a traditional religion, just like the Hindus. The Hindus, the Buddhists, and there's another one. They're traditional; so ours is traditional. We found out that our pipe is older than Christianity. But how did the Indians know? They say "father" and "grandfather," so they must have known about the coming of Christ. My father was a Christian. He died a Catholic; he is buried in a Catholic cemetery. But he still believed the Indian religion.

At one time I lived two lives, one in the Indian religion, the other one as a Christian. So when I harp like this, telling you about this, well, I feel like I am going against my religion, teaching heathen. A lot of us say it's heathen, but it's not. It is not. We knew there was a god.

But today, today this Indian religion and all religions are coming together.

I heard a story one time of an old, old woman. She prophesied. I heard this long ago. She had a grandson; he had a daughter and a son, and a son-in-law. They were educated; they were full-bloods, but they were educated, just like one of us. I have three grandchildren in California; I have a daughter in California. They live in big towns. So she (the old woman) had a grandchild that always came back to the reservation. And one day, he said in Indian, he renounced the white man's ways. He wanted to be, he wanted to study, so he came back—rode horseback, made bows and arrows and everything—oh, he wanted to do everything!

And one day the boy asked his grandmother, "Why did the white men take our land? Why did they? If they knew there was a God, which they preached to us, why do they do that? Why?"

So she said, "All right, Grandson, you shall find out yourself. And that's what we're doing now; we're going to find out ourselves. We got to do this in order to find out the truth, just like I told you. Go up on the hill and pray, meditate; you'll find out. Go down a creek and pray, and the brook will talk; even the little bird will talk to you— the truth."

So she sent him up the hill. She said, "You go up that hill. That's a long way, but you have to go up there just like you came on this earth." So he threw off his clothes, and he went, with nothing on at all. She said, "You go along; when you get on top of that hill, any rocks you get hold of, you hit them together, they spark. When they spark, you look down. You're going to see my house, my tipi. When you look down at that spark, then you'll find that sign; you'll find out."

So this boy ran. Pretty soon his feet were sore, and he went through thorns, was bruised up, and he thought he'd just as well turn around. But he stayed with it. See, that's it. That's the main point. That's the way we have to do it. He kept on. Pretty soon he felt like his tiredness was gone, so he ran like a deer from rock to rock. Oh, he jumped all over, almost like a deer. He got up there, and he picked up two rocks, and he hit them. And the flash came. Down there, below, he saw a flash, so he went back.

And the grandma said, "You go one more time, and then you'll find out." And she wrote a circle out there, and then another, and then another, then another, then another, then another. Then below this she says, "Grandson, this religion, this is the Indian religion. Some day in the future, I predict that all these churches will jump back here, and be one. Whenever that comes, there will be peace on earth; there will be no wars. When that time comes, we will understand each other. So that's what we do now."

Anyway, just like my father says, there is one man in the world; his name is "all men." And there is only one woman in the world; her name is "all women." And they have a child, and that child's name is "all children." But we never, never, never understand. Never. Even me, yeah. We're black, we're yellow, we're red, and white. And by the way, there're a lot of anthropologists trying to decipher my dad's, my father's vision. One of them says he's right. The black horse stands for the black people. The white horse—there is a horse dance in here, and the white is for the north, stands for the white man. And the east, the red man, that is the Indian. The yellow is the Japanese and Chinese.

And there is only one at the horse dance. When we get into that, there's only one horse in there; they're all going to come together.

Well, what do you say? How long did I talk? Well, as we go along, this is quite a session. You know my dad, all these books that he wrote—at first, he was reluctant about it. We Indians believe if we want to know—just like the story I told you, that boy went, took the pipe, and he went to lament. He found it out, but he never told.

Now it's up to us to find things out, but we must have to suffer, be hurt, in order to know something. In order to know something, we have to know knowledge by being hurt. And we hurt so bad that it is into us. We're Indians, and we're inclined that way. If you're an eighth Indian or a sixteenth, you're inclined; you're more inclined that way. It is so easy to understand what we are trying to talk about, and today that's coming back.

But, on the other hand, there is a big weapon on the other side; that's the white man's culture. The white man's culture has been crammed down our throats so much that, today, we forgot we are Indians. I know a lot of Indians that are ashamed they're Indians. We have a wonderful culture that we should retain. At one time, the Indian taught his children so that they didn't have any teen-age trouble at all. Well, that boy, when he became thirteen, fourteen years old—he was trained from the time he was born. We had to re-spect our mother and father, and we became warriors when we were fourteen. That's what we're trying to get you to know, so you can know what the Indian culture is, then maybe we can turn our tables.

I travel all over the world. When I was in Europe, I wanted to find out. I wanted to know; I wanted to know. So I went to places where there are farmers, and I was treated like a king. Everywhere I went, there were Indians—feathers on them. I talked to Indians that were Frenchmen; they had Indian clubs. The same when I got to Belgium. There're a lot of Indians. There're cowboys; they even hold their guns like that demonstrating, so I had to go under it. They carried me to the car. When I was in Sweden, there were about forty cars, caravans. They were all Indians, all dressed.

I found out that European people know more about us Indians than the people in the States. They study us. They study our culture; they study our history right from the start, from the schools. Well, we don't here.

I went to Washington DC, on education. I brought that up. Bobby Kennedy was alive. First time I ever saw him, I said, "You know, the white man should study us, so that we know each other better. We could figure out what's coming on tomorrow. We have to." But I should have kept my mouth shut. I said, "I know why you don't want to teach your children Indian culture and history. I hate to bring that up." One senator jumped up beside me and said, "Black Elk, if you know so much about it, why don't you tell us, show us." I said, "Look what you did to us at Wounded Knee. You mowed us down just because we wiped Custer out. He asked for it, so we got him. But you bunched us up, took all the weapons out, and then shot us down. But that's not a drop in the bucket to what you've done, compared to what you've done to the Cherokees in Georgia. You marched them from Georgia to Oklahoma, and six thousand went and four thousand died on the way. But, to top it off, your own president—I have the facts—your own president offered two hundred dollars a head for Indian scalps. You try to exterminate us, but here I am; I'm still here. Just like I said to you, I was here first, and I am still here yet."

So Bobby Kennedy took that in. That's why he came here, Pine Ridge, and he insisted on going to Wounded Knee, but that took the hope. So now, this is what we're doing, see, but I am glad to do this because I am getting old.

Last winter I went through two operations. My last one, I lost a lot of blood; they had to give me a blood transfusion. By the way, I'm not a full-blood anymore! So I prayed to the Great Spirit, "Give me just two more years, then I'd spread the gospel." I'd spread more of these; so that's what I am doing. Maybe Great Spirit heard my prayer, and here I am. I don't know too much, but what little I know, I like to share with others, so then they know.

Here is what my father said, "It is my prayer that through our sacred pipe and through this book, peace may come to these people who can understand, and understanding must be of the heart, not of the head alone. Then they will realize that we Indians knew the one true God, that we prayed to him continually."

When my father was going to talk about *Black Elk Speaks,* about his life and vision, he prayed like this: "Hear me, four quarters of the world—a relative I am! Give me the strength to walk the soft earth, a relative to all that is! Give me the eyes to see and the strength to understand, that I may be like you. With your power only can I face the winds."[9]

Isn't that great? So with this conclusion, I will say, "How, Kola!"

[Ending song.]

Father And Grandfather

Benjamin Black Elk

HILDA: You were telling how your father, Ben, would go around gathering honey. Can you tell us any more about that?

OLIVIA: He went around, looking for a beehive with honey in it. When he found one, he took the honey and brought it home. My! That was good!

ESTHER: I remember when he used to set traps for coyotes. He had a trap line, so he'd go out early and check those traps. I was home with my mother, and Grace was home at that time; she was younger and smaller. Well, every time he went checking the traps, if it was getting late, we worried about him. He'd go horseback. One morning he left, and he didn't come back, and it was getting dark. I kept looking out the window, and it was dark then. So I told my mother, "I wonder what happened. He should be back by now." This was in wintertime.

So there was Grace peeking out of the window—the back kitchen window. "I wonder if he may be back?" she said. All that time, my dad was taking off his boots out there, and he happened to step up and scared Grace. She just screamed and hollered and laughed at the same time. She was so glad to see him, and then it scared her so much she laughed and screamed and cried at the same time. We had to shake her and bring her out of it.

HILDA: What did he do with the coyotes that he caught?

ESTHER: Well, he'd skin them and sell the pelts—sell them. Even beavers—and mink, he used to trap them. We all helped take care of the cattle and horses. We never had to worry about food; we always had chickens and ducks, turkeys. And we had all our potatoes and everything in the cellar. But if it was below zero, we couldn't open that cellar, so we made sure we got enough. We didn't have to worry about food. The only things they used to buy were like the lard, bacon, coffee, and sugar. Those things they bought.

HILDA: So they needed to earn money for that?

ESTHER: Yes.

HILDA: And your mother, of course, worked at home?

ESTHER: Yes. One time in the thirties we had come back for Christmas, I remember. I was small then. I was going to school at Holy Rosary, and we came back; I think we came back with Father Zimmerman that time. I must have been about twelve—eleven or twelve.

We were decorating [the Christmas tree]. We didn't have lights, you see. We had crepe paper, and we drew our own little round things [ornaments] different ways. And then we had little pinecones, and we hung them all up. Then we made an angel and put it way up there on top. And that was my brother Henry's. We all had to make angels.

The next day was Christmas. We were sitting there, and my dad and mom sat down and said, "You know what? We have lots to eat; we have a big Christmas dinner. We have turkey, pies." We had pumpkins in those days. We had everything we could have for Christmas dinner. So my father said, "Just one thing"—and we were all listening—"we're poor. We can't have [Christmas]; we don't have any money." He was trying to tell us something.

My father said, "We can't have Christmas this time." We didn't say anything; we just sat there, quiet. Oh, we might have just a little; we had our stockings hanging up. He told us, "There's going to be just a little bit in your stockings, but don't worry about it; we've got lots to eat. We'll have a lot of fun." So we said, "All right."

The next day, we went to midnight mass. And he said, "We're not going to open our presents until morning." So we went to midnight mass, and we went in the wagon. Then we came back, and the next day—we were waiting, wondering what they were—Mother and Father were whispering to each other. Then I said, "Here, Mom took him in the kitchen. Gee, let's get up; let's go find out if there's something in our little socks." So we got up; we went in there. We didn't want to look at the socks. We ran in there and we started helping Mom cook and everything, and my dad walked in and said, "All right, you guys, we're going to open our presents." He took down the socks.

We had a little bit of candy in there and one big box; that's all we got. And we were satisfied, because we had our own homemade sled, anyway. As long as we went sleigh riding.

We had a good Christmas, and we never even thought about crying, because he had already explained it to us. Oh, it was the best. Sometimes we didn't have much. We were happy.

LORI: Aaron, would you tell us what you remember about your Grandfather Ben?

AARON: My Grandpa Ben was very kind-hearted. He was the one that taught us, him and my Uncle Henry, how to dance, up at Mount Rushmore. And there were a lot of things he used to teach us that I didn't realize were important in my life until I started carrying my pipe. He was always telling us, "Never walk backward. Never do anything like that. Lakotas don't do that, go backwards, only certain ones—the *heyókhas*."[1] But they taught us how to dance when I was small and growing up. I remember him. We used to go outside the house and he'd have his pipe stretched out.

One time we were coming from Gordon, and Grandma had packed hard-boiled eggs and crackers. I was sitting in the front seat. I was small then; I think I was in about the third grade. We were coming to a stop at the Gordon junction, at the Y corner there. Grandma pulled out the eggs, and I asked Grandpa to peel my egg. He was standing on the corner talking with Grandma, and Grandpa peeled the egg and ate it. Pretty soon I said, "Grandpa, where's my egg?" And he looked around and said, "Oh, I ate it!" So when we got to Gordon he bought me some candy.

One time Grandma was sitting there—all of us were sitting there— we were eating breakfast. Grandpa said, "Boy eats more than three pancakes, three eggs, bacon, and a bowl of cereal. Can you eat more than that? You're a pig!" So I just kind of quit.

My Grandma Ellen and Grandpa Ben, they were the nicest people in the world. They'd go out of their way to help their grandkids. My grandpa gave us all these ways that come down, but in this world, we still have to walk in our own shoes.

I have to tell some other memories I have of my grandpa and

grandma. When all of us were young, we used to go up to Keystone all the time, every summer, and dance with them.[2] My brother Clifton used to do the buffalo dance, David used to do the chief's dance, and then I used to do the eagle dance. And we were taught all these different dances—the kettle dance, the shield dance. All of us learned these dances a long time ago as we grew up.

Nowadays I see the dances, and they're different than the way my grandpa and all them taught us a long time ago. One of these days I might teach the young. The older ones in the family used to do that—like my sister Cheryl and my cousins, Cleo and Penny. All these things that we were taught—there was something special about it. And we didn't realize that these were our traditions, the Lakotas' way of doing things. We were making money to survive; we were being taught our traditions. As we got older, we understood that these things that were taught were important.

And then I remember that after every show they used to buy us ice cream, and we'd go back to the house, and Grandpa would go to work on Mount Rushmore, and then he'd come back.[3] He used to carry his pouch with a whole bunch of change; all of us used to sit there and count it all the time. There would be some extra, so he would take it and divide it up between us, and we used to go down to Halley's.

There were a lot of things that we learned, and we were taught to respect our elders. A lot of people think that we're real rich, and stuff like that, but we're not. It's that we know how to manage things in our lives, because our grandparents taught us how to do that. And the Indians a long time ago knew how to manage things. They saved what they had.

Growing Up

ESTHER: There were six children in our family: Henry, Kate, Olivia, Grace, Benjamin Jr., and me. Kate was the first Indian woman in our area to be in the WAAC [Women's Army Auxiliary Corps]. Later she was an accountant for the tribe. She died from a brain hemorrhage when they were treating her for a tumor. Benjamin Jr. died when he was sixteen.

OLIVIA: One thing I always remember about my mother is that she used to make yellow soap. We used to have to scrub our wooden floor, and the wood turned yellow from scrubbing it so much. We had to get down on our hands and knees to scrub it.

ESTHER: Our house had to be just right.

OLIVIA: We'd take turns cooking and baking. But when we had our period, we didn't have to bake.

ESTHER: We had chores to do, and we all had to take turns washing dishes. We washed them clean, and the dishes had to be wiped.

OLIVIA: Our walls were like—you probably saw them when you were there—the walls were muslin.[1] I have a picture of the log house where we were all born, and it has a dirt roof.

ESTHER: A long time ago when they washed their clothes, they used that soap weed. They cut it off, and they used that. And then they'd pound the clothes on a rock. We used to use that wash board, remember? Our fingers would be just raw. We didn't have bleach, so we had to use lye. We had this boiler, put water in there, and we'd buy lye, put soap in there, and let it go. We stuck our white sheets in there. We'd stir it up, take it out, wash it, and it turned out nice and white. We used to stand over a washboard and really scrub away.

I can remember the first washing machine Aunt Lucy had. It was a wooden machine, a wooden agitator, and you had to stand there and make it go like this [motions] and it would go around and around. We used to take turns.

OLIVIA: And then the wringer—we had to stand there and wring. I thought the machine was nice. We didn't have to scrub.

ESTHER: And then I'd say, "Your turn," and she'd say, "No, you didn't do it long enough." We'd get our clothes hung out then. And it would be so cold; you'd be hanging clothes, and your hands would be ice-cold, and your clothes would freeze solid. They smelled good when you brought them in—so clean!

ESTHER: We had some rough times. I remember when we had to pitch hay. Henry and the other boys went into the service, and it was just girls at home. So we were out there pitching hay, and then all of a sudden a snake would be in there. We'd just drop everything and run, screaming.

OLIVIA: I must have been about thirteen. We were good at harnessing up a team. And our horses—all we'd have to do is take a can and beat on it, and they'd come.

ESTHER: We used to go after mail in a wagon. We'd go horseback or we'd drive the team.

OLIVIA: When my dad used to break a horse, it'd be one of us he'd put on that horse, and he'd be breaking it. He made us into tough kids!

And then at one time we milked—how many cows?

ESTHER: We used to drink milk all the time. We didn't have a separator, so we used to just skim the cream off. And we used to make butter in a jar, shaking it back and forth. We had to take turns doing that, too.

ESTHER: We learned a lot from our mothers and grandmothers about gathering food. Years ago I think everybody respected nature—the flowers and trees and birds and animals. We did not have buffalo, but our grandparents and great-grandparents did. They used everything, even the tripe. The hide they used for tipis, and the bones for knives.

Nothing went to waste; even the hoofs were boiled and dried, and that's what they saved for winter.

OLIVIA: They took the hoof and boiled it, and they dug out the inside of the hoof for soup. And we did our own corn; we made our own hominy.

ESTHER: They took the corn and used ash wood, and they burned the wood and it had to be clear ashes. They took the ashes and put the corn in and boiled it together until the hull came off.

HILDA: How did you learn this?

ESTHER: We'd seen them do it. Mom did it then.

OLIVIA: She did the hoofs also. My pa would butcher, and she would hang the hoofs on the side of the house until they were nice and dry. Then she took it and put it in boiling water, and boiled it and boiled it, and then she slid the hoof off.

ESTHER: And then they mixed it, cooked it with hominy. They strained the hominy out of the ashes and they kept changing the water, rinsing it until it was big and white.

HILDA: Did they season the food with anything?

ESTHER: I don't think they seasoned the food with anything; they just ate it plain.

OLIVIA: They had to dry their food, because they moved around. They didn't have groceries or anything like that. They had their *pápa* —their dried meat—and dried berries, dried corn, and turnips. And then they had "greenies." We still eat greenies. It's really clover when it's real young. When it comes up, you take it and wash it and cook it like spinach. Then there were the plums. When they were real ripe, we mashed them and dried them, just like cherries. You get cherries and make *wóžapi* [Indian pudding]. In the old days, they made little bags out of hides—called parfleche—and that's what they put it in.

Everything was wild, and they went way up in the Black Hills to pick berries. We knew of a place in the Black Hills where we could get raspberries. They were real good, and you just picked them and made *wóžapi.*

ESTHER: For sweeteners, they used honey they found in trees. We were competing with the bear people!

OLIVIA: And then they had wild cauliflower. You had to pick it at a certain time. The same way with the sand cherries—you have to pick them with the wind. If you go against the wind, your sand cherries are going to be bitter.

ESTHER: The sand cherries grow on the ground in the sandhills. They're little bushes, and if you go with the wind, they're sweet. We didn't believe that when we were little, but we experienced it and found out it was true.

OLIVIA: And here's another food—*chąnákpa* they call it.[2]

ESTHER: That was in June when we had rain. There would be a long rain, four or five days of rain. *Chąnákpa* is a big mushroom up on the elm trees. We used to take sticks and knock them down.

OLIVIA: You have to catch those at a certain time, too, otherwise they're buggy. They have little grooves, and you have to wash them. If you catch them at the right time, you don't have to do that.

You take it and put it in flour and fry it. Man! You couldn't get enough of that! It's so good!

ESTHER: When they made jerky, they would pound it, and they had it in a piece of hide. They scraped all the hair off the hide, and then they had it in a kind of boat shape, and when they made *wasná* [dried meat with melted fat, sugar, and dried fruit], they put their dry meat in there and pounded it.

OLIVIA: To this day we still make dried meat. We dry meat; we dry corn and make cherry patties. It's harder to dry meat now, because there's too many flies. In the old days, why weren't there flies? How did they keep their meat so clean? It's bad now; the flies are really bad.

ESTHER: When they had hard times, they didn't get enough food. Still, the men would go out and hunt, and as long as they had meat, they were all right. I guess we all loved meat—rabbits and pheasants and grouse. When they dried their meat, they had a certain way of cutting the meat so it wouldn't fall apart when they hung it up.

And then the cherries—sometimes they just spread them out and dried them whole, instead of pounding them. They did that with grapes also. I remember our mother had a box, and she put a thick layer of grapes at the bottom. Then she put paper, and then another layer of grapes, and that's how she dried them. When they were dry, she put them in bladder bags.

There's some certain part of the intestines they used for fat, and they rendered the fat and they put it in there, and it would get hard. And they used to make something stuffed like wieners. They took the intestines and cleaned them, then stuck the meat in there, tied each side, and cooked it that way.

One time my mother was doing that, and my brother Henry came along with a fork and poked it, and that thing just streamed up in the air!

ESTHER: When we sit back, we kind of reminisce, thinking of those things we did. We had hard times, but still we enjoyed it—always laughing and running and doing things together. It was a hardship, but we still did it in a way that we were happy and laughing and teasing each other. Sometimes you have family problems, but we were taught to overlook things and talk things out. That's the way we were taught. We were told to respect each other and to help each other. And that's what we do.

Olivia and I would go some place, and they'd say, "Here comes—
OLIVIA:—the Gold Dust Twins, because we did things together.³

LORI: What kind of games did you play?
OLIVIA: You mean the Indian games that we played? The hand game —how does that go now?
ESTHER: You have little sticks (or rocks); one of them is red in the middle, and the other one is plain. And you have to see who can guess the red one. They have a song that they sing in Indian, and then they go like this with their hands. [Hands move back and forth sideways, the two hands coming close together in the middle, then each hand moves quickly away and back to the side.]
OLIVIA: They throw it back and forth.
ESTHER: Their hands are quick, and then one has to guess which hand the red one is in. It's just a game and a lot of fun. Sometimes at different places they have bets; I don't know what they bet—horses

or whatever. There are people who are quick. It looks like they're just swinging their hands, but they are transferring it from one hand to the other. And then they open the hand that the person picks.

OLIVIA: And if the stick is red, then that one goes over to the other side, isn't that it?

AARON: Until they get all the sticks.

ESTHER: There's usually four on one side and four on the other side, together. They flip a coin to see which one goes first. And then the one who wins—how is it now? If one wins, they step aside?

OLIVIA: They're out of the game. Like if I was against you, and I select the red one, then you go off. And then you pass it on to the next one. The side with the most people remaining wins.

ESTHER: And then they have another game. They have hoops of different sizes, crisscrossed with leather thongs. And they have sticks, kind of like spears. The different sizes of the hoops go from big ones to small ones. They throw the hoops, and you have to throw that spear, hoping it goes through. And they count how many players miss or fail. Some of them are pretty good and get the spear in between the thongs of the hoop. But that smallest one is the one that gets you.

OLIVIA: Another game is almost like hockey.

ESTHER: Yes. They have a ball, and they have sticks with a hook at the bottom. They have a goal, and if they hit the ball in there, they get a point. It's like hockey.

AARON: Hockey and soccer mixed.

OLIVIA: I often wondered if they [white people] got their soccer games from us, because in our games they also kick. They would kick the ball, and then they would kick it back over here, and kick it again.

HILDA: What did they use—a stone or what?

ESTHER: Rawhide made into a ball.

AARON: They'd take a bunch of hair and stick it in there and wrap it with the hide of the buffalo.

ESTHER: Buffalo hair, or whatever.

AARON: They even use it in one of the ceremonies—the last ceremony of the bison.

ESTHER: I already told you about how the children play with their horse and wagon and doll. But the grownups are like that, too. They play the hand game and that game with the hoops.

ESTHER: We played games, but the most fun was riding horses out in the hills. At that time, my father had cows, and we used to have to go look for them. We'd have to look for them and bring them back. We knew all the places where the cattle would go.

OLIVIA: One time Esther and I went up on the hill, and there was a crevice in the ground, and we found some shells—little white shells that the Indians wore on their dresses. They were kind of washed out of the ground, but we didn't know it was a grave when we found the shells. We came home and found a jar and went back up there—we were on horseback—and we picked up all those white shells. We didn't dig a hole or anything; it was just washed out of the ground.

ESTHER: We took it back to the house, and—

OLIVIA: Papa came home and—

ESTHER: Bawled us out silly!

OLIVIA: He made us go back and put it back where we found it. Then he got a shovel and covered it all up. Now I can't even remember where it is.

ESTHER: We used to ride all over. My mother would say, "Be careful!" and everything else. She didn't want us to ride sometimes, but we'd go. We'd do our work and get it out of the way first.

Marie Jumping Eagle—she lived near us—and my sister Kate and I used to ride all over in the back. There are a lot of graves, and we knew just where the graves were. So one day we were going and we took a different route. In the springtime, especially just in June around here, it's nice and green, and it's beautiful, and especially in the valley into Manderson. When the sun goes down, our white buttes look pink, and we used to watch that all the time.

This time we were up in the morning when we left, and the girls said, "Let's take a different route." So I told them, "Okay, we'll go this other way, but we're going to have a drop gate." A drop gate is all fenced straight across. We'd usually carry a hammer and we'd pull all the nails out, push down the fence, and then we'd take our horses across. So Kate said, "Marie, you stand on this side, and Esther you stand on that side and hold the fence down. Then I'll lead the horses across." So she led the first one and the second one, but the third one's hoof got caught between the wires. He lifted his foot up and the fence came up with it, and we went flying—Marie went that way, and I went this way and was knocked out of wind. I happened to look, and Marie was just lying there. She wasn't even moving, so we went over and just shook her up, and she came out of it; she was just knocked out of wind. So the horses were already across, and we got back on our horses and away we went again.

And then up in the hills we saw different graves up on the hill. And then we went behind Grandma Bluffing Bear's place and rode up on that hill, and there were four graves up there. We went to Grandma Bluffing Bear's to find out whose graves they were. She said they were her relations, and that was her allotted land.

We'd go down those hills and cut across the road and then the other way—east, and way back in there you see a tombstone.

AARON: It's a mile north of Wounded Knee. The tombstone says Crow Scout on it. It has the day he died, and the day he died was the same day as Wounded Knee.

ESTHER: And when we came out from that ride, we came down, right across our place.

We used to roam all over on horseback. Marie would come and say, "I'm going after mail," so then we'd all go—my sister Kate and Marie and I. There used to be a wooden bridge; now it's a culvert in the creek. We'd pass that, and we'd look back, and if we couldn't see the house, boy, we'd race to see who got there first! But we'd never let our mother know, because she'd think we'd fallen off or something. We used to do that all the time.

We used to go in the wagon, visiting Grandma Hanska (hąska). My Grandma Good Shell was in the place where we're living now. I was small then. My mother always had little aprons on us. We had to wear aprons with little pockets. Everyone used to call her Grandma—Grandma Hanska. She was tall—hąska means tall, you know. We'd stop there and visit, and I remember a girl—her name was Margaret—we used to play at home with her and we cut paper dolls. She had little scissors. Once when I got home, I reached in my apron pocket, and the scissors were in there. My parents said, "You're not supposed to steal," and they took me all the way back, and I had to give the scissors back. I was cutting; I stuck it in my pocket, and I didn't know I had it until I got home.

HILDA: Good Shell was your grandmother? I remember her. We have a picture of her. She was good to you?

ESTHER: Oh, yes, she was. She was little; she was short. I used to go all over with her.

I remember I used to stay different places. I don't know why I always wanted to go and stay with different relatives. One day I went back with Uncle Johnny and my mother's brother. They had buggies a long time ago and I used to like to ride in the back, so I went with them. And the next day, I walked back home from Uncle Johnny's. That must have been a mile away. And then I went to see my Grandma Good Shell, and she was right where we lived together.

OLIVIA: Years ago, the Indian parents were overly protective. They taught the children right from wrong, right from the beginning. Nowadays it is different. That love between parent and child is not the same, and the way the kids behave is different. In the old days, there was nothing there for them to do and be raising Cain with. And that's when the parents were right there to protect them, and they showed a lot of love. Now there is no love in some of the families. I worked with children, and you could tell it, just by the way the children acted.

The way I see it, there is a lot of difference between the love then and the love now. I worked with children from kindergarten to eighth grade—I was in guidance—and we had to take a psychology course about working with children and with parents. Our mom and dad always loved us and hugged us and put us near them. Nowadays babies are in a carrier and are carried around in that, not held near the parents.

But the elderlies don't believe in that. They feel that the child should be held and be near you, and the child feels that. I worked with children, and I know the parents did not show them much love, because when I wanted to hug them and show love, they kind of pulled away.

ESTHER: When we were little, we always played together. We made our own dolls and other toys and played together. Nowadays, the children have plastic toys, and it is just not the same. We did not have much, but we did things together, and we really had a happy time.

School Days

OLIVIA: When we were little—I was five—we were stuck at that Holy Rosary school. I went to school twelve years. We never did get to see Grandpa too many times when I was in school, but as I got older, in my teenage years, that's when I knew Grandpa. Nineteen forty-seven was my last year there.

We were in real poverty then. We had a hard time. My folks couldn't afford to buy us shoes, so then we had to wear school shoes. And sometimes the nun would give us short shoes, and we'd have to wear them. And that would hurt. We had to wear uniforms at school. They were like cotton, all the same color.

ESTHER: We had to wear aprons on top of them when we first started school. We had our dresses. We used to call them mission clothes.

OLIVIA: We couldn't take them home.

ESTHER: When we'd go home, we'd have to put on our home clothes.

OLIVIA: Sometimes I grew so fast that my home clothes would be short on me, and I'd have to go home in clothes too short!

ESTHER: When I first went to school, I went in, and it was on a Friday. I don't remember which nun it was, but she said, "Well, today is Friday; you have to go downstairs and go to the bathroom," down there where they take their showers. I turned around and looked at her, and said—we were taught to speak, and I knew some English—"I took a bath this morning already." She grabbed me and said, "Go ahead and take a bath again." I can always remember that.

Every time we'd come over the hill in a wagon to the school, Olivia started crying. She really let out a yell; it was real loud. She didn't want to go to school.

OLIVIA: One time we stayed there [at school] for Christmas, because my folks couldn't afford to come and get us. Everybody went home for Christmas, and there were maybe five or six that stayed there. Everybody got a porcelain doll. We all got dolls in boxes. I opened my box, and here was a little colored doll. The other dolls were all little white dolls, and mine was the only little dark doll. I felt offended. I felt, "Why me? Why give me a dark doll?" And do you know what I did? I just buzzed that thing clear across the playroom! I didn't want any dark doll. Sounds crazy, doesn't it? It just popped; it hit the wall, and it just popped, and the little head and everything scattered.

And I got punished for that. I couldn't go to recreation; I had to stay in the playroom. One of the sisters made me some flour dough; you know how you make the paste. I picked it all up and pasted it [the doll] with that flour dough, and I tried to put it back together, because everybody had a doll, and I didn't!

ESTHER: We had to do work part of the time at school. We were all assigned to clean the kitchens, dining room, dormitory, classrooms. We'd work, and then in the evening we had benediction. On Sunday we went to church in the morning—about ten or eleven o'clock we had High Mass—and then in the evening we had church.

OLIVIA: Church again! We went to church three times on Sundays.

ESTHER: Other days we went to church twice—in the morning and in the evening. We used to say we had "church knees."

OLIVIA: That's why our prayers didn't have meaning, because we memorized them.

We just said them and said them. We memorized it all.

ESTHER: Even our Latin.

OLIVIA: I took two years of Latin, and it's not doing me one bit of good. I don't know why I did it. I was forced to, that's what I would say.

ESTHER: I took two years of Latin, too, but some of your English in the dictionary is Latin. It helped me where I worked.

OLIVIA: Our mattresses were made out of cornhusks, and we had to make our own mattresses.

ESTHER: They'd give us bags and we had to stuff them with cornhusks.

OLIVIA: And we had wood stoves. In the morning it would be so darn cold. Sometimes we'd sleep with our clothes on because it would be so cold.

ESTHER: And after we'd get up and wash, we had to fix our beds nice, and then the workers came in and put shams on the bed. The shams had HRM on them—Holy Rosary Mission. They were blue, and we put them in the starch.

OLIVIA: Do you know the way I feel about the Catholic school? They knocked prayers in our heads, and we memorized them. I could answer the Mass in Latin, but there was no meaning to it for me, because I didn't understand Latin. And I never could. I knew that saying prayers was praying to the Lord, but I never really ever went into religion until after I retired and moved home. Then I picked up the Bible, and I pray now in my own words. In my own words, because in the Bible it says that the Lord is with us continuously, no matter what we're doing or where we go, he said.

And it's just like the Indian religion. The Great Spirit is with us constantly. We have all our own spirits, and the spirits of our loved ones are around us constantly. And that's how our ceremonies take place, because when they have a ceremony, the spirit doesn't talk to the person that talks to them; it talks to the spiritual leaders.

Mourning and Teaching

OLIVIA: He was a fancy dancer, my younger brother, Benjamin Jr. He must have been about sixteen when he died in 1948. My mom just gave everything away when my brother died. My dad went to the Black Hills on horseback to mourn, and I even have a picture of him with the travois. When he went through the Black Hills, the tourists took pictures of him. He even went up to Mount Rushmore and down to different places, and he came out over here at Buffalo Gap near Hermosa.

HILDA: And why did your father go on horseback up in the Hills?

OLIVIA: The Indians believe that when you lose a loved one—now, like my brother Benjamin—the spirit went up to the Hills. Benjamin traveled around through the Hills as a little boy. He and my dad—all of us—went there. My dad said he was going to look for Benjamin's spirit, follow the places where he went.

There's a belief that when you go away out in the prairie someplace, and you have a little boy with you, or a little girl, on the way back you have to call them—call them by name, so that they'll be with you. Because if you don't, when that little boy or girl leaves the world, that spirit is going to still wander around in that area where they went up in the Hills, or in the prairie, or wherever. I don't know if the rest of the Indians believe that, but we do in our family, because of my granddad. He's the one who told us these things so we could understand.

I mentioned it one time to a lady at a meeting, and she told me, "Yeah, we do, too. Like when you go cherry picking," she said, "coming back I call all my kids' names, because I don't want to leave their spirits over there."

So that's why my dad went to look for my brother, his son—to follow wherever my brother went, and to call him. We call it "wandering to mourn." Wherever my brother went, our father backtracked. About four days in the Black Hills he traveled all over, with a blanket on his saddle on the horse. He probably slept out on the prairie or in the open. But he was satisfied when he came back.

At Mount Rushmore, the tourists started taking pictures of him. They asked him if he could stand there with his regalia. And he said he would, and so they said they'd pay him. Well, he came back all excited, so we all moved to Keystone and they started taking pictures. He was up there twenty-seven years. That's where I got all these pictures.

HILDA: When he was up there, being photographed, didn't he also tell a lot about your own religion and ways?

ESTHER: It was mostly Indian lore, Indian history, going way back. Tourists would come and ask him questions about it, and that's what he did.

And then he went to universities, rotaries, and spoke. They called him from different places. He said he first checked the people out to see what age group they were and then he'd just talk to them, tell them whatever they would like to hear.

OLIVIA: And then during the wintertime they would ask him to do lecture tours to different schools. The schools would pay him.

A Life for the Community

Esther Black Elk DeSersa

ESTHER: When I was small, I always played that I was helping people. We had dolls, and I used to wrap their hands and pretend they were hurt, and I was nursing them. Remember Kate and the doll that you dipped in a bucket?

OLIVIA: I took Kate's doll. I was so jealous of her, because I didn't have a doll and she had a doll. I was just little, so I took that doll and stuck it in the water. Esther was standing there and saying, "Poor little sicka doll." And every time she'd say that, I'd dip it in again, and Kate was standing there and just screaming, trying to get her doll out of the water.

ESTHER: So after Olivia took it out, I dried it. That's how I used to play, to be a nurse and help people. My grandfather would say in the Lakota language, "So you want to help people?" and I would say, "Yes," and grandfather would say, "Well, that is the way you'll go, then."

But I never once thought then of being a nurse. I went to school at Red Cloud—Holy Rosary. I went there for twelve years straight and graduated. I was valedictorian. At that time we had to write our own speeches and then we had to memorize them. Nowadays they just write the speech and read it. I was up on the stage, and I was looking around to see if my mother and dad had come in. I didn't see them, so I started to give my memorized speech. All of a sudden, I saw my dad come in, and I lost it. So I just made up my speech after that.

After that, I went down to Oklahoma and trained to be a nurse, a licensed practical nurse. I had to work my way through to pay for everything. I worked in a cafe, and I was only getting seventy-five cents an hour waiting tables. That was the first thing I ever hated. I hated waiting tables, but I had to do it.

Then, after my training, I came back and worked in Klamath Falls, Oregon, among the Indians. At that time I was only nineteen, and I was getting one hundred dollars a month. They called it a nurse's aide then, but I was really a licensed practical nurse. They do about the same things as a registered nurse does. You give shots and all that. I got my license and worked in that field in hospitals in different places for about fifteen years. Then we went to Chicago, and I worked nights as a scrub nurse.

This was after I got married and my husband was going to school. I worked nights, and he'd go to school and work part-time. We only saw each other about three or four hours a day. We didn't have a baby-sitter—the kids were all little—and I worked nights and was home with the children in the daytime. And when I was working at night, he was home with the children. So that's what we did until he got through with his schooling. He went to barber college first, then to Loyola University.

I'm telling you, I didn't like that place, Chicago. It was no place for children. I worried about the children all the time. Even when they went to school, I was worried. When they're home with me, then you know it's different.

I worked in the same Norwegian Hospital, and then I switched to St. Joseph's Hospital, where I worked in delivery. I am not sure of the date—1960, 1961, 1965? Anyway, I worked with all different nationalities. And finally I got another job up north, at Swedish Covenant, a private hospital in Chicago. I don't know how long I was there. It's a religious hospital, you know, and they don't smoke. At that time I was smoking, and we'd go clear down to the basement to smoke, and then we'd only take three or four puffs and then go all the way up again! So finally I quit.

We had hard times. Sometimes I'd make bean sandwiches and take them to work at night. It took me one whole hour to get to work on the bus.

My husband didn't finish school, because his dad was always sick.

We always had to come back here, and it cost too much money, so we decided to move back to the reservation.

First I worked at Mission, South Dakota, in the grade school there—part time as a nurse and part time as a kindergarten teacher. I was going to school at the college in Vermillion then. One of my duties was to screen the kindergartners. They were mixed, Indian and non-Indian. This is one of the things you did: you told them to pick something up from under the table, or jump up and down. Little things like that. And then I'd write it down, their names and what they did and what they understood. That was psychological testing. I noticed that the grades of the non-Indians were high, and the Indians' grades were lower. I thought about it, and then I turned it around. I took the Indian children one at a time and asked them the same questions in the Lakota language. And do you know they did everything. Their scores were just as high as the non-Indians. You see, our own language is first; English is our second language.

So then I went and showed the principal the records I had made of the Indian children. He asked me, "Is that true?" I said, "Yes. They're just as smart as those other kids. The little kids understood what I said in Lakota. It wasn't a matter of intelligence; it was just a matter of understanding the language." And I got an A+ on that!

I worked next at the Indian hospital,[1] and then at the credit office for about two years at the BIA [Bureau of Indian Affairs] office there. Then I ran for council in Wounded Knee District. I got the most votes, but when I went to the council for certification, they took me off [the list of candidates] because I wasn't living in Manderson. So I took a half-day off from my work and went to the council meeting where they were doing the selection of officers. At that time they were nominating a secretary from the floor, and one man nominated me for secretary of the tribe. I was surprised and said, "Oh, gee, I couldn't do that!" But the man who nominated me said, "Just leave it in; just leave your name in there." "Okay, I won't get it anyway," I said.

So they voted, and the two highest votes would have a run-off. It was just this man, who had been secretary for many years, and I. They said that we would first have to do some campaigning. Instead of campaigning, I just went around and shook hands and talked to everyone, said "hello" to them, and I never said anything else. When they brought up the vote, do you know it was ten and ten? I thought I would not get it, because the other man had been secretary for so many years. But pretty soon they broke the tie and I was secretary of the tribe!

That was in 1970 or 1972. We lived in Pine Ridge then. I accepted the appointment, and at the first meeting there were three resolutions to be introduced. At that time, the secretary had to write up the resolutions, but nowadays they don't have as much to do. I had taken speedwriting, so I had everything written down the way they wanted it, what was supposed to be in the resolutions. At lunchtime, I went back home and asked my husband, "Can you help me with these three resolutions?" Do you know what he said? "You accepted the appointment. You learn the best way you can."

I am glad he said that, because I did learn. It was hard, though, because I typed all the resolutions. We used stencils then and didn't have copy machines, so things would be purple. Now there are three or four people working in that office. At the meetings, I'd be hurrying up, taking down the minutes. Afterwards I'd be sitting there reading my speedwriting to my secretary, and she'd be writing it down in her Gregg shorthand. Then she'd type it for the mimeograph.

I was secretary of Wounded Knee District for thirteen years. In 1979 I quit being secretary. I told them that there were younger people that would like to do it. Then this year they had a meeting and nominated me once again. I got up and made a speech. I said, "I was secretary of this district for thirteen years before, and all the people I was secretary to—the chairmen—are all gone. They're not here." So then I said, "I'd like to be secretary one more time." When the voting came up, I got more votes than anyone else.

I was also secretary of the St. Mary's Catholic Congress for eleven years and president of St. Mary's Catholic Congress one year.

In 1969 my husband inherited a newspaper. We did not know beans about journalism, but my husband had an uncle who ran the paper, which was called *Shannon County News*. His uncle was sickly, and before he died he told his wife, "If you cannot run this paper, give it to my nephew." And that's how my husband got the paper. We changed the name to *Crazy Horse News*.

My husband and I didn't know anything about journalism. There's another thing we had to learn the hard way! My husband wrote an editorial and I always wanted it corrected. "No," he would say, "leave it that way. That's the way the people talk." He always wanted the editorials left that way, but it was okay to correct the rest, like the news. My husband did most of the writing. He took the ads, and they paid by the inch. I worked in the evening on the paper, and I worked for the tribe as secretary.

Every one of the children helped. We all did. As a family, we kept the paper going. We didn't hire anyone else. We all did a lot of typing, pasting, putting it all together, and taking it to Rapid City to have it printed. The money came in, and we just put it back in the paper. We didn't pay each other, because it was small and it cost quite a bit to put it out.

The last paper my husband wrote was in 1981. He was so ill. But I still have the paper, and I can open it anytime I want.

ESTHER: We moved to Rapid City, and I worked with Indian education. When we moved back home to the reservation, my husband told me, "Well, we're not going into politics. We're going to stay home and retire and do nothing else." You know, though, when we came home, pretty soon there he was already busy. So I went to work, and he went to work, and I worked with this health service, where I am now.

So after we came back to Manderson, we raised our kids, and they had to finish school. After they finished high school, it was up to them to decide what they wanted to do. When my husband was in the hospital, he said, "We have only one [child] yet to go to finish high school. If I don't make it, I want her to finish high school." So all of them graduated from high school, and that last one was Honey Bea. She was only a junior when he died, so I kept that promise.

You see we both just sat down and decided that our kids were going to have to finish high school. At that time, when you finished high school you could always get a job in an office or something, because you took typing and shorthand in high school. But now, for these programs—directors or assistants or accountants—they have to have a degree. There are some that get in with a high-school diploma, but then you can only be something like a receptionist, some little job like that.

So education is the main thing nowadays. And I can always remember my dad saying, "We have to have education to compete in the white man's world." I am happy to say that all of our seven children have some college education, too. They all attended South Dakota State University in Brookings, except Honey Bea, who went to Huron College in Hudson, South Dakota.

ESTHER: I'm not being paid now for my work at the Indian Health Service. We brought eight programs in, and the council took every one of them. The council said, "Go write up a different program." I asked, "Couldn't you write one up? It should come from the council." It's been held up now. For over a year now we haven't been able to get a Public Law 93–638 program. [The Indian Self-Determination Act gives Indians the right to run their own programs with federal funds.] We get money from the tribe or the Bureau of Indian Affairs or social services. I guess there is a cut in the Indian Health Service now. We have a good relationship with them, but most of the time we work with the hospitals. There are a few non-Indian people who work in the BIA, but mostly Indian people work there.

So that's what we do. If different programs come and they want to modify a budget, then I sit down and help them do that. And proposal writing—if they need help, they usually call and ask me. The proposals would be for a grant or foundation, for money to help them with their work.

We are still working and donating our time. There are three of us here—Irma Bear Stops, Arta Carlow, and I—the others already have other jobs. I have worked with Arta Carlow since 1970, and we are still working together and donating our time. We were paid for a while, when we had funding, but the tribe took our programs away because they needed the money.

The Health Authority is a different entity from the tribe. Our board has nine members, and they meet every first Friday of the month, with special meetings at other times. I am in the office and I have a secretary, and then there's an accountant for the payroll. When we began, it was as a health planner program. Then we received money, but right now we have none. The tribe took all the programs, and they are using the money for indirect costs.

But we're still existing here in Pine Ridge. Pine Ridge is the seat of the government. If the people have some kind of problem, they come in and talk to us. If they need their house fixed, I tell them they can go to the housing department. If people come in with their bills, we just call the right department and tell them to go over there. If nothing is done about it, the people come back to us, and then we go or I take them to the contract officers. If they need water, I show them how to get that. If they need something for their house, if the roof is leaking or something, then we go to the housing department. If people need help going places, or if they have someone who is really sick and they need to go to the hospital or a doctor, we help them get there. If they come in for burials, then I help take care of that and send them to the right department. So we work with all people on the reservation. I was involved in the new hospital facility we have in Pine Ridge, also with the health center in Kyle. Arta Carlow and I did the groundbreaking ceremony for both buildings.

HILDA: So you're just helping people that come to your office?

ESTHER: At least until we get a few dollars in there. Do you wonder what we're doing? We're selling lunches at noon hour. We have a lunch sale, and that's how we pay for our telephone and utilities. We have a little room, and we have a microwave and a freezer and a refrigerator, and then we bring our little frying pans or electric skillet, and then we make pot roasts, stir-fry, and Indian tacos—things like that. And then we sell them. We do it on Thursday. All we do is put up a sign out there, telling what we're going to have that day, and then make sure it's on loud, colored paper. We've got pink now so they can see it! So whatever we sell, we use to pay our bills.

Reclaiming the Legacy

Olivia Black Elk Pourier

OLIVIA: I have two Indian names: one name is Echo. When you stand up on a hill and holler, it echoes back. I said, "Maybe that's why I am such a big mouth now!" My Grandmother Mestez gave me an Indian name, and it's "Sings After"—Wicaglata. My Grandmother Black Elk gave me the name Echo.

OLIVIA: I quit school in 1947. I finished at OCS at Pine Ridge—Oglala Community School. I only had a month to go, and I quit because my mom got sick while I was at school. I went back one year after that. Then after Mom got better, I went to Rapid City for three years, in 1948, 1949 and 1950. I worked the night shift at Kraft Bakery.

I came back to Manderson, South Dakota, in 1950 after my grandpa passed away. I didn't go back to Rapid City because I met Hobart Pourier. Hobart's first wife had died of cancer. I was a real good friend with one of his daughters, and I came back to see her. After his wife passed away, well, then he had the two little ones. One was three going on four and the other was five going on six, and I just fell in love with those two little ones. Gee, they were cute kids! And so I took care of those two kids—I'd take them home and bring them back, and finally Hobart said, "Oh, hell, why don't we just get married? You've been with me all this time." So we got married in 1951. I raised five of his kids, and he had ten children. With our one, Curtis, that made eleven for him.

From then on I made my life with Hobart. He died in 1993. He and I were married forty-one years. Whatever I have today is really what Hobart helped me get. I always said I was raised with his kids. He was my husband and father and everything.

I was way younger than Hobart. He was twenty-three years older than I was, so what I learned, I learned from him. I worked side by side with him. When he went out to fix fences, I went with him. When he went out to feed [the livestock], I went with him. And I even drove a tractor. We planted spuds and we had a potato planter, and I sat on the back of the planter and pushed the potato through that hole and planted potatoes. So I know how to work out on a place. His kids had a lot of respect for him, because he was a stern man. What he says goes. That's the kind of man he was. But he was a loving guy. And the kids really loved him.

When Hobart was alive, I never made coffee in the morning, and after he died, I really had a time in the morning! Now, here I was going to get up in the morning and have coffee, and no coffee made! That's one time I really missed him.

His grandfather was Baptiste Pourier, a Frenchman and one of the scouts.[1] He spoke Indian fluently for a white man, and then he married a full-blood [Indian]. Well, actually I don't know if she was a full-blood or not, but she was a Richards. Hobart was only about one-fourth Indian. They adopted Old Man Pourier—Baptiste Pourier—into the tribe.

After I got married, I didn't see my folks that much—just when they came to see me. They came quite a bit, because they liked to be with me. Of course, my hours were so crazy when I was working, but I kept my folks quite a bit; I really did. I always had an extra room for my mom and dad. They had nothing at home anymore, because all they did was travel. They were living at Manderson, right behind Esther's house, back where Grace lives. There's a little log house. It's a three-room house.

Hobart and I both worked for the government. Hobart taught at the big government boarding school at Pine Ridge. He taught horsemanship, taught students how to ride and how to take care of horses. Oh, they had beautiful horses there! They had stallions, and they had Morgan horses. They did everything themselves. They had poultry, they had their own dairy, and they taught the kids how to do things—vocational classes, they called them. They taught children how to put up hay and all that, but they actually did it for the school.

I worked at the school, starting out in the laundry department. But before I could work for the government there, I had to take a ten-hour test to get my GED, my diploma. Hobart and I went to the state college at Chadron, and that's where I got my GED. Hobart already had his diploma. We both worked for the government, transferring to two places. We also worked in Allen [South Dakota] at the American Horse Day School, where I worked as an assistant cook and he was a bus driver.

During that time I worked just nine months and my summers were free. Every summer for about three years I worked at Mount Rushmore at a café while my dad was up there and when Curtis was just a baby. Then in the fall I went back to work again. I was about twenty-four or twenty-five years old. Hobart kept Curtis at home. Sometimes he wanted to stay with his grandma, so that's why I know that Curtis can understand a little bit of Indian—a little bit of the language—because he used to listen to his grandma.

And then in 1956 we came back to Pine Ridge. At Oglala Community School I worked as a matron of a dormitory and later on as an instructional aide. We had kindergarten through the eighth grade in the west wing, and in the east wing it was the ninth to the twelfth grade. I was on the little girls' side—the west wing. Hobart and I scheduled our work for different hours. My regular hours were from six to ten in the morning and from six to ten at night. At six o'clock in the evening I had arts and crafts with the children until it was time for them to go to bed.

I had learned to do beadwork and quillwork, too, when I was growing up. My grandmother, Maggie Mestez, used to do quillwork so I just picked it up along the way. When I was teaching arts and crafts, we made Indian outfits. I had the girls make their own dresses, and we had a little dancing group in the dorm.

I already knew how to sew, to use a machine and everything like that. I had done a lot of sewing for my kids and for the step-grandkids. I had crocheted quite a bit, and I made many afghans.

Every summer they sent us to summer school to get college credits, so I have almost two years now of college credits in psychology. We had to take psychology, because we worked with children. We also took training in Al-Anon for the kids who had alcoholic parents. We had to teach them how to cope with their parents if they were alcoholic.

I worked at the school—OCS at Pine Ridge—for sixteen years. I worked with a lot of kids. Now when I see the children, they're so surprised to see me. Sometimes [when I see one of them] I just wonder, "How many kids do you have?" Sometimes I say to a child, "Now, which one are you?"

My job was really interesting, but I had to quit when I got paint in my eye. I have only one good eye. A lot of people can't tell it. I have one eagle eye. I can really see well with this one, the right eye. I got paint thinner splashed in my eye. It hurt; it really did. Boy, I really suffered with it! That was in 1979. I quit for a year until my eye got better. I did not go back to teaching again. Hobart and I both retired from government work. I got a disability, a retirement, pension.

Then Hobart and I moved home to this place in Porcupine. We moved back a little at a time, beginning in the spring of 1976 or 1975. There were no trees around here, but we'd buy trees and plant them. Hobart and his boy built a barn, and then our son Curtis built a house.

HILDA: What about the land here? When we went up on Cuny Table in 1931, we were told that your grandfather and your father owned land there. Do you still own land on Cuny Table?
OLIVIA: No, I owned that land, but I traded it to the tribe for where I am now.
HILDA: And you have 320 acres? So your husband didn't have anything to do with the land where you live now?
OLIVIA: No. Our house was built by the Housing Authority in 1980 or 1981, and we lived in the house for fourteen years. The time before, I lived in government housing. We first lived in a trailer while they were building this house. When they got done, I sold the trailer to Red Cloud Indian School. It was a nice doublewide trailer and they used it as a classroom.

Our family is like a village here. I'm up on the hill, and I have Natalie with me. Right below me, across the road, east of my place,

I have Duane living there. I've got Steve right up on the hill, Gary down here, Pat here, Sonny over there, Delbert here, and Edna back there. So at night, all the lights are on. Curtis lives right behind me, at the end of the road. Curtis's house is really nice. It's a home-ownership house. That means you pay, and when you pay it off, it's yours. He has a basement with utilities, two bedrooms upstairs, and a big living room. I keep telling my kids that they have land, so they have to do something with it because of the future.

HILDA: What do you think they can do on the reservation?

OLIVIA: Well, for one thing, all my children are working. They all have good jobs on the reservation. Delbert, Hobart's youngest, works at the clinic in Kyle as a supply clerk, and he has his own office and everything. Phyllis works at the clinic and she's a secretary. Carol worked with credit at the [Pine Ridge Indian] Agency, in the land department. She is about ready to retire. Duane worked at the hospital for the Indian Health Service in Pine Ridge until he was hurt, so he is on disability now. Pat is retired; he worked for the government road department for many years. He is home now, but his wife, my daughter-in-law, is very sick, so they can't go anywhere. I have a daughter, Lavonne Richards, who works in a hospital in Oregon as a nurse.

I have a son, Lester Pourier, who is an artist. He worked in California, in Santa Barbara, for a good many years. He does a lot of Indian art—painting and everything. I'll have to show you some pictures of his work, because he is really good. He lives in Rushville, Nebraska, now. He did the drawing for Hobart's tombstone. It's really pretty and is a horse with hounds around the horse.

OLIVIA: After I had retired, I got restless. I started sewing and making stuff, and I did crocheting, too. I made pillows and stuff like that. Finally, I went to find work and there was a job opening for a Lakota arts-and-crafts teacher. I got the job and worked there for about two years. I taught the Lakota language—my language. I had all the classes, kindergarten to eighth grade, and I taught traditional art.

Lakota was my language. When I went to Holy Rosary School, we couldn't speak the Lakota language or we got whipped. Shoot! I got punished a lot of times for talking my language. But my dad said to us kids that we weren't supposed to talk English when we were at home. He used to say, "Now, I want you to keep your Lakota culture and I want you to speak Lakota. I don't care what—you speak it! Don't be ashamed that you're an Indian, because I don't care where you go, you'll always be an Indian." So when we were at home, we spoke the language with my mom and dad. Up to this day, I still talk the Lakota language with my sisters.

I surprise a lot of people who come here. As soon as I start talking in Lakota, well, they just give in. They start talking Lakota, too, and they get really friendly. I didn't teach any of my children the language, and I'm really sorry I didn't. But, as I mentioned, I guess my son Curtis does know a little bit, because he stayed with my dad and my mother quite a bit as a little boy.

And now I live here in this little house at Porcupine and I have my great-granddaughter, Natalie, living with me. My house is on the flat. I don't have any steps to go up. My house was built in Norfolk, Nebraska. It is modular and came in two parts. I have three bedrooms, a very nice place, but now I have built onto it. I have my quilting machine in there, where I do my quilting. It's a twelve-footer. And then I have my front room, which is a little shop. I have the showcase in that room and I have another showcase that Curtis got for me. I make some money in the shop, but just through the summer months. During the wintertime I make key chains and doilies, medallions and other things to sell in the summer. During the wintertime I do a lot of quilting. When somebody dies, people come and bring the top and bottom for a quilt, and they ask me to put it together for them and to put in the background.

Way back, after the white man brought material and beads and stuff, people started to make their own things. Of course, we never had material or anything in the old days. But when people did get it, they really made use of it. Now they do a lot of patch quilting. They almost had to do their own quilting, because they couldn't afford to buy quilts.

OLIVIA: I have six grandchildren: Myron, Curt, Cody, Cash, Natalie, and Wiley. I have four great-granddaughters: Myron's daughter, Whitney, age ten; the twin girls, Myranda and Maryan, age nine months; and Curt's little girl, Sabrina, who is one year and six months. Myron, Curtis's son, is the oldest; he's twenty-seven. Curt is twenty-one, and Cody is twenty. Cash Coe has just turned sixteen, and Natalie is fourteen. Natalie is named after Mom, because her middle name is Ellen. Cody has the middle name of Dell. And Curt, we called him Babe Curt. He's named after his dad.

Curt's a wrestler and he went to the state competition in Sioux Falls, South Dakota, a couple of years ago. This is his last year in school now, but he's going on to college. Cody is a bull rider and he's going to join the marines. Cody rides in rodeos. Oh, it just scares me half to death! I don't even like to go to rodeos. I had two step-grandsons that were killed in rodeos, and my step-granddaughter, her husband got kicked in a rodeo. He was a good rider, a saddle-bronc rider. His name is Howard Hunter and he's in the regional hospital right now. He's having therapy because he was kicked in the back of his head and was paralyzed. Now he can't walk and he can't move one of his arms. This happened in Crow, Montana, in August of 1995. He's coming out of it, but very slowly.

I have ten stepchildren, and they're just like my own kids. The oldest one has just retired from a government job and she lives down here where I live, in a trailer across the road from me. Her name is Edna Pilcher, and she lives by herself, but right now she has a grand-daughter who stays with her. Edna watches her kids, because her granddaughter works at the hospital in medical records. And then I have Pat. Pat lives right across the road from me, and he's not working. He's kind of retired right now.

OLIVIA: It's kind of hard for children today to get into things like they should. I'd advise kids to "get in gear" and try to do something for themselves, because in the future, times are going to be different. They need to know these things [the traditions and arts of their own Indian culture]. They need to keep our culture going and to speak the

Lakota language. When I was teaching some of the good kids, they understood the language but they were shy. And then some of the little Lakota kids did not understand the language and I wondered why their parents didn't speak it to them.

Right now I would really like to train somebody to do quilting, because it's wearing me out. I'm getting too many quilts and I can't be in the workroom all the time.

I am trying to get a museum in honor of my dad and my grandfather, a place where I will have artifacts and books and tapes. Some white people are trying to help me get financing for a museum building. I've got a lot of *Black Elk Speaks* books, and they just sold out. The tourists are really coming back, you know.

I have my little shop here, and when tourists see that sign on the road, Black Elk Heritage, they just scoot right in here.[2] When they see the pictures of my dad and your dad, John Neihardt—those big pictures—they can't believe that we exist! I also have a picture of my grandfather with the war bonnet on and one of Big Bat Pourier, my husband's grandfather.

In my shop I have earrings made like dream catchers, and I have eagle-head earrings and quillwork earrings. I have bow ties and all kinds of little button earrings that I have made. I also buy things from local people. I have beaders and quillers, too, who do the work for me. But it's getting to the point where I might have to give up this part, in order to keep my quilting going. I ship a lot of quilts out.

It is possible to make a living on the reservation, if a person has the ability and the determination. I think a person can go a long way, if they have the know-how. I've heard a lot of people—tourists—asking, "Is there a café nearby here?" or "Is there some place we can sleep?" So that's the way we need to go in order for us to make any kind of money. Folks have the land, but it is not easy to get the money they need to start a business.

Tourists come to my shop and ask about the book *Black Elk Speaks*. When these people ask what I get out of the book, I say, "Do you know, if it wasn't for this man—and I point to your dad's [Neihardt's] picture—the Black Elk name wouldn't be where it is today. Nothing.

Nobody would know anything about us and my grandfather would have died with all that [left unsaid]."

I tell people that, because it makes me happy to hear a tourist man or woman say they got a lot out of that book. They got a lot out of that book, because it came from the heart. Everything, everything that is told in that book was sacred. And I tell people that. We have to think about our lives—how did we get here and where did all this come from? And we have to show a lot of respect for our country, where we are. You can't just step over something and think nothing of it. You have to look, you have to be, and you have your mind.

You have to know what this is all about. And that's what I keep telling the people. I can speak out and defend myself.

OLIVIA: My kids are all going traditional. Some of them are dancing, some of them are in sun dancing, and some of them are competing in powwows. My kids are all going traditional. As for me, I have my shop and my museum and I'm doing it because I'm thinking about the future. It's the Indian culture that I'm promoting.

The Honor of a Pipe

Aaron DeSersa Jr.

AARON: I can't remember much about when I was small, because I had rheumatic fever when I was six. I'll let them talk about that first.

ESTHER: When Aaron was little, we lived in Chicago. He went to parochial school there when he was only five or so. Once one of the sisters came to us and talked about him, saying, "I don't know what I'm going to do with this boy. He's always doing something. When he gets through with it, I give him more work, and when he gets through with that, he torments the other children. And then I don't know where he got the gum; he had gum all over the radiator and it was hot. I don't know what I'm going to do with him. I don't know; I've tried everything." While she was speaking, Aaron was sitting in a little rocking chair we had. I asked, "Do you have a library in your classroom or something? When he gets through with his work, set him over there and let him look at the books."

So she tried that, and she came back and was all happy. So after that, when Aaron got through with his work, he was sent over by the books and he didn't bother anybody.

AARON: After that I went to Catholic school, Holy Rosary, in Red Cloud. I remember in third grade in Red Cloud we used to get in trouble all the time, and I got swatted on the hands. It used to hurt, but we young guys, we thought, "We're Indians—we can take the pain." Sometimes rulers would break on us. That would hurt, but we took it. One day, we didn't want to stay there, so we ran away. And they caught us. And when we ran away again, they brought us back, and then they had the older guys shave our heads bald. Years later, we were dancing the traditional dance at a powwow, and the guy who cut my hair came by, dancing. I said, "Hey, remember when you cut my hair bald? Now it's all grown out. What you gonna do?" That was a joke, and we all laughed about it.

It's an experience going to a Catholic school, you see, because everybody says they live their lives in a good way. But they're humans —there are lies and there's mistreatment. People don't realize that. Just because they wear that robe and carry that cross and that Bible, doesn't mean they're good all the time. Now the world's finding out this truth, because there was child abuse at a lot of those places. We had a prefect that would go to the dormitory and make the kids take off all their clothes and kneel in the aisle. He said, "It's to air out your underclothes." Pretty soon the Indian kids got fed up with this. Two seventh- and eighth-graders got hold of some knives, and they chased him to his room, locked him in, and wouldn't let him out.

It all started at Catholic school. A lot of these Indian children, all they had were priests and nuns to learn from, and a lot of them turned out to be pretty rough—a lot of them. The last of my high school years were a lot better. They had teachers in the school who had degrees, and the kids had a wider choice of role models. That's when we got our new gym, and it was a lot better. Nowadays, teachers down there are not nuns; they're trained teachers.

I went to school down at Red Cloud until fifth grade. For fourth grade I went to school in Chicago, and then I came back. Then I went to school down in Rosebud; I don't remember the name of that school. Most of my school years were spent at Oglala Community School. I graduated from the eighth grade at OCS, then I went to high school at Red Cloud. It was run by Jesuits. I didn't care for that school.

That's why now I have a tendency to go the Indian ways. When I was in Catholic school, everything was forced on us. They didn't give us freedom of choice. We were punished for little things that we did. That wasn't right. If we just barely looked over on the girls' side in church, they would make us sit in the aisles, holding Bibles in our hands. And they made us stand by the wall, facing the wall, if we did something wrong.

Like a lot of Lakota boys there, we were reckless and we played rough. They didn't understand it, but we were growing up to be men.

They didn't understand our ways, and they didn't take time to learn our ways. What they wanted to do was instill their ways in us and civilize us. Now today, they still haven't civilized us. We still believe in what we are. There are a lot of our people who are highly educated, but they still live their ways like the Lakotas did a long time ago. They still believe it.

Like our grandpa said, education is our survival now. We have to have education to survive in the world out there. In the Lakota world in the old days, we were surviving; we were doing well. But now, when our family has to be fed, we have to learn things like the white people.

So I did. I went out in the white world and I survived, and I came back to the reservation. A lot of people who work in my profession don't realize that it's harder out there than it is here on the reservation, because out there, if you make a little mistake, they'll fire you on the spot. Here they give you five, six, seven chances before they let you go, and it's easier.

When I came back here, I tried to tell our people that. This isn't the way it is out there. You've got to learn and educate yourself about that fact. Book learning is not everything. Words—you can read a book, and you think you understand it, but the living of that life is different. No matter what the book says, living the life, all your life, like we do, is completely different.

AARON: In the military, I was what they call a courier. I took things to places and then back. I was assigned to the Eighth Infantry Division, and I traveled all over. I was stationed in several places in Germany in Eighth Infantry Division. I got hurt when I was in the service. A gas grenade blew up and it burned my face, and they couldn't stop the infection. It would come up on my face, and it still does today, and so I was going in and out of hospitals in Germany. They were giving me antibiotics—five hundred milligrams of the antibiotic. Then when I was going in and out of hospitals, they assigned me to the second brigade of the Thirteenth Division. I spent three months in the hospital, and I was stationed in the Thirteenth Division for about ten months. Then they reassigned me to school. They retired me in 1975, and I came back to Manderson.

Then I started school in Brookings and was living there, studying political science at South Dakota State. After I went to school, I worked for a construction company out of Denver. I worked for them for quite a while, then came back here and worked at Kyle. And that's when I started to work with Christopher Sergel on the play he wrote called "Black Elk Speaks." I lived my grandpa's ways all the way through it.

After Christopher Sergel died, the pipe of Great Grandpa Black Elk's, that Aunt Lucy had kept, came back to the family, back to my mom and my Auntie Bea.[1] It was given back to them, so they in turn decided to let me take care of my great-grandpa's pipe. They called me into the room by myself, and they said, "Well, this has come back, and you know more about it than anyone. You take care of it." So they gave it to me to take care of for the family, and for the knowledge and understanding of it.

That was a great honor that they bestowed on me, and it's a great undertaking. Today the men are not as strong as they were a long time ago. I can't walk in my great-grandfather's shoes; I have to walk in my own. I have to live in two worlds: in the Lakota world of being and in the white society, to survive.

I'm grateful that they have done that to me. It's a great honor that both of them think enough of me and respect me enough to allow me to carry the pipe, to take care of it, and maybe someday to use it. I finally came to the realization that I had to change, so I changed. My aunt and my mom right now are the most important people in my life. They're the elders, and they've got a lot of people who respect them and know them from all over. Not just on Pine Ridge Reservation, but from all over. There's nobody else in the family that's more respected than they are.

That pipe was passed down. It was my great-grandfather's pipe; it was meant for the people. I have to take care of it, because it was meant for the people. I have to take care of it because it was his learning that is on it.

On the Front Lines

Clifton DeSersa

HILDA: Clifton, when you were in school, what happened?

CLIFTON: I remember standing in line once, and a prefect took this one kid outside in the morning during breakfast, and got this big metal pot that they cook oatmeal and stuff in. The prefect took the kid's hand and pressed it up against the pot and burned the back of his hand.

They did a lot of things like that then.

Other things went on, too, when I was little. If somebody did something and nobody would own up to it, and the prefect wanted to be mean, he would just come down the line in class and take the whistle in his hand and hit everybody on top of the head—all up and down in the class. Until one time my brother got up and swung it out with him, and then my dad went down there and chased the prefect all over the place.

Those guys were all studying to be priests. The sisters—I don't have much to say—they were all nice. I never knew a nun to be mean, unless you teased her or something, and then she'd chew you out.

When I went down to Holy Rosary and learned the language and everything, one priest whipped you for doing it wrong, then he up and quit the order and got married. They were beating us while we were at school, and then telling us to do right. And we would always wonder, you know, whether every priest that you talked to was right or wrong, whether he lied or not. A lot of them say priests don't lie. They aren't supposed to lie and cheat. But that's hard to believe nowadays, too.

I ran away from school one time and got whipped and taken back to school, and they whipped me at school, too. I didn't run away after that. When you catch it from both ends, it's pretty hard to do it again.

Kids today are old enough where they think they can do whatever they want. They know they can get away with it. A teacher can't holler or even correct the kids in the school system. When I went to school, if you didn't do your work, they'd scream at you and make you do the work. They'd stand right there and watch you and send you in to the principal, and they'd whip your butt. Just skip class or something like that, and they'd whip you and send you back to class.

CLIFTON: I was just a year old when my great-grandfather [Nicholas Black Elk] died. I knew my grandpa, Ben. Every summer we—myself, my older brother Byron, my sister Cheryl, and my cousins Dave and Cleo and Penny and Angie and Emeline—used to go to Keystone and dance and perform during the evening time for all the tourists. We stayed at my grandfather's place. He had a small house up there with a bunkhouse where all the boys stayed. It was kind of small, but when we were little, it looked big.

All summer long he and my Uncle Hank used to sing for us while we danced and performed. It was a way of showing the tourists the different styles of dances that we dance, and it was just another way of making money, too. We just passed the hat, and they'd give us money—donations and stuff for our performing. We did the buffalo dance and a shield dance—two warriors would fight all the time with the shields. Byron used to do the hoop dance and the eagle dance. He just about knew all the dances. And then we did the kettle dance. That's where you put a pot outside, and in the center they dance. It's kind of hard to describe. We did that for a few years.

ESTHER: You go back and dance toward the kettle. A long time ago the kettle was supposed to have soup in it—meat or whatever. And that's how they danced to it. They'd eat the soup after the dance.

CLIFTON: See, that's how it was supposed to be, but when you danced and performed it in front of the tourists, it was different than the original way. It was the same way dancing, but—

ESTHER: But there was nothing in it. It was just a dance.

CLIFTON: I was twenty when I went in the army, and I was in for three years. We went into a bar with a recruiter, who asked us what we wanted to be if we joined the army. I told him I wanted to be a heavy-equipment operator—mechanic. He wrote it down, so we thought we were all signed up then. We all thought we were going to get what we asked. I took my training at Fort Polk, Louisiana. When we finished with our training, it turned out different. When we came back on leave, we came looking for that recruiter. But he was gone; they transferred him out.

After Fort Polk, there were different schools you could go to. There were four of us that went together—me and my older brother and two of my friends. My brother went to noncommissioned officers' school, and the other one, he went to special services, so he could play guitar; he played in a band.

My other friend and I decided to try the airborne. I went to Fort Benning, Georgia, for my airborne training. It was kind of scary at first, because we went jumping out of those towers. We also jumped out of a plane quite a few times. You get way up there, and you stand in that door and you look down—see those trees down on the ground, about an inch high down on the ground. And they tell you to jump. Well, the first time, I just closed my eyes and jumped out. They've got a steadying line that you hook up, and then you jump out the door, and it pulls your chute automatically. Then they've got a reserve chute that sits out in front of you. It takes you down if the chute doesn't open. You count to three—like one thousand, two thousand, three thousand. If your chute doesn't open in that time, then you'd better pull your reserve.

There were a couple of guys that broke their ankles—depends on how you land, you know. Those were the old parachutes—the old T-10 parachutes—so you couldn't really control them half the time. The new ones they've got nowadays—they say you can control them up to ten miles from where you jump. But the old T-10s you couldn't. You had to almost jump right where you wanted your people to land, because you couldn't float that far with those chutes. The other kind, though, you could maneuver them all over in the air.

Jumping was fun; at least I thought it was—after the first time I did it—and then the second time, it got easier.

I didn't jump when I was over in Vietnam. I was in infantry. Everybody was on guard duty. You just slept whenever you could, and that was it. Took turns sleeping for about an hour, hour and a half. We lived in bunkers, in sandbags. That was your home for a year. The countryside was mostly jungle, but part of it was rice paddies. Once I was wounded with shrapnel, from a grenade.

In my unit, I think I was the only Indian—in my company, anyway. I know that there were probably Indians scattered all over there.

We used to have this little kid, a Montagnard. They live way up in the mountains. They're different than the Vietnamese people. They're like the Indian people over there. They use crossbows and stuff. And this one kid, he used to bring us ice, and he used to have a comic book with cowboys and Indians. He asked me if I was an Indian, so I said, "Yeah." Then he said, "Well, me and you is the same thing." And I said, "No, I don't think so." He was still a pretty good kid. That's the difference between the Montagnards and the Vietnamese people: the Montagnards didn't like the other people. They were kind of like a different tribe; they were way up in the hills. A lot of them were used as interpreters and stuff like that over there. They helped the Americans more than they did the Vietnamese. Most of the time you didn't think the Vietnamese were on your side.

CLIFTON: I got discharged from the service in 1972, just before the 1973 occupation of Wounded Knee.[1] I was involved in quite a bit of it. I took a lot of news reporters and my dad over the hills into Wounded Knee. We went to the creek bottoms and took a bunch of news reporters—there must have been about twelve or fourteen—from different newspapers from all over the place that way. Took them over the hills that went into Wounded Knee.

ESTHER: In the first place, my husband was a newspaperman. And that's the reason why all these newsmen came to the house and asked my husband to take them in, and he didn't want to at first. There was a whole bunch of them, about twelve or fourteen—they all came in with their packs. There were some women, too. They called it the

AIM [American Indian Movement], but my husband and my children were not AIM, they were [part of] the Civil Rights Movement—they usually helped the people. And so he finally decided to take them, and Clifton went with them.

CLIFTON: We took the reporters in, and we stayed in there for a little while. After we took them in, they [AIM] got news media coverage and announced a lot of the leaders. Then the following day my dad and I left, taking a different route out of Wounded Knee into Manderson, and then from there I went back to Pine Ridge.

On the way in, one of the reporters dropped part of his camera that kept it from working—his battery pack or something. He went back all by himself all the way out there to find it, and then he came back to Wounded Knee. He must have had an awful lot of guts to go out there to find it and then come all the way back, and not run into anybody out there. On the way in there, we made the two women reporters take off their high heels. We told them they weren't going to make it, wearing those shoes, especially over the country we were going over—the creek bottoms and stuff.

For me, it was just like an adventure going through something like that! I went into Wounded Knee, I'd say, about six or seven times in and out.

We were taking some packs in one night and we came up over the hill, and it was dark, and we sat down to take a break. And all of a sudden a police radio came on, and we were sitting right down there in front of the police unit. We didn't know it was there, and we had walked right across in front of them, and they didn't see us, because it was dark. So we just got up and snuck on down the hill and took off. I had our big dog, Duke, with us, and I guess he tried to attack one of those marshals, or whoever it was, so they ended up shooting at the dog.

ESTHER: The dog would protect them when they would go in.

CLIFTON: All he'd do was run circles around us when we were going in—just like there was coyotes. We were going over the hills at night, and he'd just run circles around us. That's his territory. And when anybody tried to do us harm, he'd end up taking on somebody before we'd get caught.

They later shot the dog. Well, the dog was kind of mean, anyway. They just pulled up to the house, and they wanted to come search the house, but my little brothers were holding on to that dog, and they were kind of scared of that dog, and they didn't want to come too close to that dog, because it was pretty mean.

LORI: Was everyone positioned so you could avoid them, or did you just take your chances and try to avoid them?

CLIFTON: I don't know. I had been born and raised there, and I'd been all over the hills in Manderson, so I kind of knew where to go and get in. We didn't know where the FBI or the National Guard or the regular BIA cops were positioned a lot of times. There were a couple of times when a helicopter came over the hill—could have cut us off— but I had learned an old army trick when I was in the service. When a helicopter is up in the air, and if you just stand still and put your arms down, and you stand in the brush, they can't tell what it is, whether it's a person standing there or if it is a tree. It's just like me using my training against them, and they were just National Guard people. And there were quite a few of us that were in the service that were in there at Wounded Knee.

HILDA: How many people were there when it was occupied?

CLIFTON: There were quite a few people there. They've got a picture book on Wounded Knee, and it shows that whole store and stuff, and the people that were in there. But that isn't all of them. There were quite a few other people that were in there. But I had fun, running from the cops. I worked with my dad as a reporter.

HILDA: You feel that you should not mention the names of any of these people who were in there with you. Why is that?

CLIFTON: Because I don't want to get in trouble, and I don't want them to get in trouble.

HILDA: You still think you'd get in trouble?

CLIFTON: No, I don't think they can do anything to me nowadays about what happened a long time ago. I think it's all over with.

ESTHER: It's a neutral zone now.

CLIFTON: Yeah, it's all over now. Put it in the past.

After Wounded Knee, I went to different occupations all over the place. I went when they took over at Custer [in protest over the death

of a young Indian man]; I went over there. But we went in as reporters, with my dad, with the paper. In Wisconsin we went up to
the abbey when they had that takeover [when the Menominee tribe
occupied the Novitiate Seminary that had been built by the government on Indian land]. I went to Seattle when they were fighting for
fishing rights. Then I was on that Longest Walk to Washington. After
my brother got shot—my older brother got shot and killed—I kind
of gave up on it.

CLIFTON: Beginning in 1972 I worked for the legal aid with the Pine
Ridge court system. The court system is a lot different from any other
court system off the reservation. A lot of times, if you had relatives in
the court system, if you got in trouble, then you could easily get out
of trouble, because of their being related to you. Off the reservation,
it wouldn't be that way.

The tribal council selects the judges, and the tribal council is se-
lected by the people, every two years. They have a primary election,
and in March they have the general election, and in April they take
over. Right now we have twenty members on the council. Before, it
used to be more than that, but the referendum changed it. The council meets in Pine Ridge. They take it up to the districts now. They have
a meeting in one district, next week they have a meeting in another.

ESTHER: There are eight districts plus Pine Ridge, which makes nine.

HILDA: When you worked with the tribal court, did you help people
accused of some misdemeanor?

CLIFTON: DWIS [driving while intoxicated] and stuff like that. If
somebody like that got put in jail, I went to court and represented
them in court. It's a lot easier to work than it would be in a different
court. A tribal attorney doesn't need a degree or anything to work
as tribal attorney in our court system. Anybody can go in and buy a
license and represent somebody in court. Quite a few times I represented a lot of people in court—for DWI, custody hearings, and getting children back when they're off the reservation, divorce court,
and stuff like that.

HILDA: Custody—that's a hot topic now.

CLIFTON: Yes, it is. A lot of places off the reservation, like in Colorado, they don't want to give the kids back.

If people were living in the city, and they went out and got drunk or something, welfare would take their kids away. And then welfare doesn't want to give them back, see? So the parents turn around and go to the reservation. The reservation intervenes and takes custody of the kids. Then the parents go back to our court system, and our court system turns them back over to them. A lot of places off the reservation are fighting this system now, because the tribe just turns them right back over to the parents again. Some of them might be right, but again some of them might be wrong.

HILDA: Are you working with the tribal court now?

CLIFTON: No, I am not.

CLIFTON: In 1976 I worked as a juvenile officer with the juvenile court on the Pine Ridge Reservation with children from all the different schools. I worked mostly with problem children that were involved with alcohol and drugs and stuff like that.

We had a couple of kids that we took care of. And then when they were in trouble, they used to go to school from the jail. Then after school, they'd come back to jail. When I was doing that, it changed the kids, so that after while they didn't want to be sitting in the jail. They ended up staying in school and not running around, raising Cain.

But nowadays they don't do that with the kids any more, because if you do, right away they call 9-1-1 and holler child abuse. Most of the time by following the way the system is set up now, you can't tell your kids what to do without getting in trouble. If you spank one of them, then you get in trouble with the court. You can talk to them, but then you can't tell them what to do, like [you could] a long time ago. When I was going to school, if I skipped, I got whipped. And even the school would whip you a long time ago.

HILDA: Is there more of a problem with drinking than there used to be, or is it getting better?

CLIFTON: With the younger kids it is more of a problem now, with them drinking and smoking dope and stuff, than there was a long time ago. A long time ago they were stricter than they are nowadays, because of the laws.

CLIFTON: About two years ago, some guy in Sioux City was going to make a bunch of postcards. He was taking old-time pictures to make the postcards. He didn't want to get any kind of roads in the picture, so we went way back in there. I was riding a horse, and he was taking a picture. We stopped and talked for awhile. He said, "You know something? Is this supposed to be a long time ago?" I said, "Why's that?" He said, "Well, you've got glasses on." So I had to take my glasses off.

So then we fixed it. He had a camera set up, so he reached out and got more pictures of me riding the horse. We didn't have a bit for the horse. You can hardly stop him. We just had a regular halter on, and he took off on a full lope, and I couldn't stop him. He went up the side of the hill. I slid off, because we didn't have a saddle, only a buffalo robe on that horse. The buffalo robe slid off, and I dropped off the horse.

Part 2. Lakota Past, Present, and Future

Working

HILDA: Aaron, you've mentioned that your friends say that just because you work for a living, you are living the white man's way. Can you talk about that?

AARON: Welfare was not the Indian way. A long time ago, the Indians worked to get their food and to make their tipis and all that. They were hard workers, but during the period in between, let's say, 1950 to 1980, the ones that grew up on the reservation got lazy. And they live off of welfare, and they say, "There're not enough jobs for us out there." There are. If they would go out and look for jobs on the reservation, they could get them. There are jobs there, if they could do the job. But people are so into being poor.

The Indians are really clean people. I've seen old houses where they used to have dirt floors, and they'd sweep it and pack it down. They used to hang white linen. They'd wash it and keep that white linen around the house clean. Nowadays I see a lot of laziness, and even I accuse myself of doing that sometimes. I realize it, so I get up and start doing things. And I work—for six years I've been working real hard.

All these things that are here made them lazy. And it's also because of the drinking problems on the reservation. A lot of people say, "Oh, I don't have a drinking problem." But they do, and they don't realize it.

HILDA: Are your people doing things to help those who drink too much?

AARON: Sometimes you can't help anyone, because they don't want the help. I don't try to say, "You're doing wrong," or anything like that. When they're drinking, I just sit there and let them drink. They have their lives; they have to choose. They have to learn how to choose. They are still good people. They treat people nice and everything, but they have no respect.

ESTHER: We do have a place that helps people, in Kyle, South Dakota. It's more for alcohol, though they're thinking about drugs now, but not doing much yet. They have counselors to counsel them.

HILDA: Is it helping? Are they being helped?

ESTHER: Some. I think it all depends upon the individual. When some of them go to have treatments, they come back, and they fall right back in the same way. It's their environment—when they are having treatment, it's all right there, but they start drinking again after they come back here. I think each individual is different.

HILDA: Do you think that, overall, it's getting better on the reservation?

ESTHER: No, I think it's still the same. This reservation is supposed to be a dry reservation, but now there's more alcohol on this reservation.

AARON: In our treaties that outline our borders, it's still federal law that the buffer zone is ten miles all the way around the reservation. It is a federal law, but still the state of Nebraska is violating that federal law by having a town—White Clay—selling alcohol, beer, wine and all. It's just right on the other side of the reservation line. It's the only one. That's why you see Scenic, and you see Interior, so far from the reservation. Both [towns] were started a long time ago when that federal law was still being upheld. The state of Nebraska is violating that law by allowing them to have liquor there in White Clay. It's violating the law that Congress passed and ratified. A lot of people don't realize that. When the tribe tries to stop it, the courts rule against them.

HILDA: Has the tribe tried to stop it at White Clay?

AARON: Several times. They even have walks, protest walks to White Clay, because of the alcohol they have. But they don't have jurisdiction, because of the state line that separates them. In a criminal matter, federal law supersedes a state law, and this is a federal law that has never been changed. Nebraska has not honored that law for years. The U.S. government should make Nebraska close it down.[1]

HILDA: But the problem won't be cured until your people decide what you personally have decided—when all your people decide that, or most of them. Do you think it's getting better?

AARON: It's fifty-fifty. There are a lot of young people that are turning to the Indian way. Sometimes they fall back into it. Today, my generation, we're not as strong as our grandpas were in the Indian way. It has to renew itself and give us a sign.

HILDA: The other day you said that you are bringing back the pipe and the old ways, but even so, you can still work and earn your living.

AARON: On the outside.

HILDA: Do you feel that's what your people will have to do in the future?

AARON: The future of our people is to be able to create, to make an environment on the reservation so that all the people can work. A long time ago the Indians did that. Our grandpas did that. They raised cattle and had gardens, and then they traded food and everything—cattle, horses and all that. And there were means for survival. Today it's not like that. A lot of them are in government housing, and they don't have anything to trade. They want food stamps and welfare, and when they get that, that's all they live on. They don't try to feed themselves or go out and look for land to live on, to raise a garden or to raise cattle, pigs, even chickens for eggs. They get food stamps and they run to the store.[2]

Welfare helps them out when the little ones are growing up—fine. But they should instill in those little ones the right ideas. The little ones see all this and they start catching on to that way of life. When they get older, they live it; they start having kids, and then they go to welfare. They should learn that a long time ago our grandpas worked hard. They cut alfalfa and they pitched hay; they had horses and they had chickens. I remember when my dad used to put in a garden. He put in a great big garden, and all us boys had to work. We'd pick it, and Mom would can and freeze. Some of it would be left over, and he would take and give it to the old folks at Pine Ridge.

If all the people would start doing those things again, people could survive, and everybody could live in a good way all the way through. Until that starts again, what was there is lost.

With the old ways, all families would pitch together and build a home for the ones that were growing up. They all lived close together or they lived in the same place, and the kids grew up. Dads and uncles helped raise the kids. That was in our family, too, because our Uncle Hank and others used to correct us and teach us. In our family today that's the way it is. It isn't in every family. Still, down on the reservation there are certain families that keep this way going.

The tendency is for people to say, "Oh, you're living the white man's way." But if you look at it, *they* are living the way the white man wants them to live. Our ancestors a long time ago lived the way they wanted to live, and that's what we [in our family] are doing. We live the way we want to live. If we want something nice to watch—a color television—we go out and earn the money to get that television and put it in. In order to survive out here, to get things like that, you have to earn the respect of storeowners and get the credit ratings that you need to do all that.

But nowadays a lot of people don't want to get that job. They don't want to get that credit rating. So they say to us, "You live the white man's way." But that isn't true. When our grandfathers wanted something in their home, they'd get it. Even in their tipis. If they wanted a good buffalo robe, they'd go out and get that buffalo robe. If they wanted food in the tipi, they'd go out and hunt, bring food in there; they'd gather. They'd do it themselves, without having to depend on anybody. They said, "Remember the helpless ones." In the *thiyóšpaye* [extended family] they would come back with things and help the helpless ones. My mom, she's seventy-one years old, and to us she's that way. So whenever she wants something—she has good credit, she can go and get things—but when she wants something, we get it for her. And when a member of our family is having a hard time, she would help them out. See? That's creating a circle that always comes back to her: if she treats somebody in the family good, that one would treat her the same way. People don't understand that, and when you try to explain it to them . . .

There are still some on the reservation that have not split up from the old ways. My Auntie Grace lives right in back of us and my cousins live over on the other side. They have a little *thiyóšpaye* on the other side. Auntie Kate lives by that creek, White Horse Creek. And whenever they have to do something like branding or fixing fence, all of them get together and do it for my Uncle Carl. That's the same way with us. Whenever Mom needs something, we all get together and do it. That was the old way of life, and the life people are living now is what the government is pushing on them. They don't realize this, and they think that being Indian means you have to live like this. But they don't. They don't have to. If they want to be Indians, they have to learn to work together and live a *thiyóšpaye* way of life.

All of us have a tendency to stop and help each other out. When my brother Sherman wrecked his pickup—rolled it—he didn't have a way to get another. In order not to just give it to him, I said, "I bought a pickup. Well, Sherman, I'll sell it to you for the same price I bought it for." So he paid me for it, and that's helping him out because he didn't have it like I did. Then it came back around when my engine went out in my four-wheel drive, and he turned around and gave me an engine and put it in that four-wheel drive. See? That's working with each other.

Once we went to Gordon, and I was sitting there and Mom said, "Well, I have to buy a freezer, a deep freezer." And I said, "We'll go out and look for it, and we'll talk to Charlie about it." She was prepared to buy it herself, you know. I asked, "Do you want the deep freeze?" She said, "Yes." And I said, "I'll buy it for you. It's yours." And I bought it for her and paid for it and gave it to her, because she helps everybody out. So that's the way the *thiyóšpaye* works.

HILDA: What does *thiyóšpaye* mean?

AARON: Extended family.

ESTHER: A little community.

AARON: What they call a band of relatives that stay together. In the old days, they made their kill, and they would bring it back to the families. If they had excess meat, they would give it to the helpless— the ones that couldn't hunt. That's the way of the *thiyóšpaye*.[3]

AARON: In the old times, Indians never did depend on the government for homes and stuff like that. Nowadays we think we have to because of the way society is. But we don't really have to. They could go out and look for jobs. There aren't that many jobs at Pine Ridge, but there are some, and they could go after them. There is a construction company right now that is contracting out all their work. Indians could go after those contracts and put other Indians to work. But they're scared to, because they've been spoiled by this "give me, give me" from the government. Our tribal government is also that way—they want money from the government, but they don't know how to create their own enterprise. With all this money that comes down from the government, if we had some true leaders in the Lakota sense, they wouldn't just have blown it on workshops and stuff. They would have put that money aside and built something—bought land back from the Black Hills—and started it so that the tribe would become a nation again.

But there are no true leaders in our society now. They're all little bitty leaders. There are no great leaders like they had a long time ago that stood up and talked for the people. Sitting Bull, Crazy Horse, they negotiated with the United States government as an independent nation, nation to nation. That's the way we were a long time ago, and now we don't have any leaders that will lead the people in a good and right direction.

You see the ones fighting in court trying to get the Black Hills land back.[4] But the United States government is never going to give it up. The only way the Indians will get that land back is if we buy it back. Use the white society's ways to buy it, to get it back. That's what's good. They say, "Take what's good out there and use it." And you learn that. And what's bad, throw it away. They could create business for the Indian people, and the Indian people could be out there trying things and creating their own economy for themselves, instead of being hopeless on the reservation. They could become a nation again. We've still got the richest arrangement from the government, because we've got trust status—the land that the tribe owns and that the tribal members own, who come back on the reservation, isn't taxed. The state and the federal government can't tax it, and according to federal law, it hasn't been changed.

Benjamin (Ben) Black Elk, ca. 1959. Photo by Robert Savage. Courtesy of
Charles Trimble.

The Black Elk family, ca. 1945. *Back row (left to right)*: Grace, Olivia, Esther, Katherine. *Front row (left to right)*: Ellen, Ben, Nicholas ("Black Elk"), Benjamin Jr., Henry. The woman and child in the doorway are unidentified. Courtesy of Olivia Black Elk Pourier.

A new generation of the Black Elk family. *Back row (left to right)*: Henry, Ben, Nicholas Jr. *Middle row (left to right)*: Olivia, Ellen, Bertha. *Front row:* Nicholas Jr.'s daughters Virginia and Theresa. Courtesy Olivia Black Elk Pourier.

(Opposite top) Home of Ben and Ellen,
Pine Ridge Reservation, ca. 1925.
Courtesy of Olivia Black Elk Pourier.

(Opposite bottom) Ben Black Elk,
wandering to mourn. Black Hills,
South Dakota, 1948. Courtesy of Olivia
Black Elk Pourier.

(Above) Oglala Sioux tribal office,
1950s. Courtesy of Hilda Neihardt.

Esther Black Elk DeSersa and Olivia Black Elk Pourier holding Black Elk's rosary. Courtesy of Hilda Neihardt.

Black Elk on Cuny Table, 1931. Courtesy of Hilda Neihardt.

HILDA: Now, are you saying that if they took the money that they won in the law suit, which went on for a hundred years—and it's on deposit—if they took that, are you saying that they could buy back the land?

AARON: No, if we had money, we could buy land that is up for sale up there in the Black Hills, and then put it back into trust.

LORI: How would they do that?

AARON: I had a scheme a long time ago, but nobody would ever listen. Buy up all the land around the national parks and then gain control of the national park services. And when the national park services didn't have the money to maintain it, the Indian people [could] start maintaining it.

HILDA: I understand that some Lakota people are strong in regard to not taking the money. Is that right?

AARON: Yeah. It's because they believe that because of that treaty they could get the land back. People are also afraid that [receiving the money from] the judgment would cause us to lose our trust status. We would lose everything underneath taxes. So that's why they didn't want to take the money.

But what they're doing is, they're beating their heads up against a brick wall. They'll hit that brick wall as long as the government is there. I went to school and studied political science, and I know that brick wall. You learn in college that you're either a part of that brick wall or you're not. If you're not, then you'll keep butting your head against that brick wall and you won't get anywhere.

The Indians have never been a part of that wall before. Their heads butt against it, but that wall is not physical, it's mental. It's a mental wall that was established two hundred years ago, and that mentality was strong. It took a German to start knocking down that wall in Germany. It takes an Indian to knock that mental wall down here, but he has to be smart enough to do it. We have learned all these years that the government has not lived up to its promises, and it never will.

The Indians keep butting their heads against a brick wall. I learned a long time ago that once you hit a brick wall, just leave it alone and go around it. And the Indians haven't done that. They keep hitting that brick wall, and that wall's the U.S. government and Congress. The only way is just to go around it, to use their system on how to get the land back.

HILDA: Maybe you can have some influence.

AARON: Will people listen, though?

The Use and Misuse of Lakota Religion

AARON: I'll talk about these things for this book. Maybe somebody among our people will look at it and see the truth. That's why I am going to tell it, so the truth can be heard.

I'll tell you how our Indian religion started over again—the way I see it.[1] A long time ago when they started persecuting the Indians for their religious beliefs, everything was hidden in the background. But one year these three elders got the right to bring our sun dance back.

Those three elders went to Manderson and got the Elkhorn pipe, the one used in the last sun dance out toward the Bad Lands. They brought the pipe to Pine Ridge and one of the three was supposed to take care of it. When they started the sun dance, they wanted to bring traditional religious ways back to the Indian people. Because of the government restrictions, they had the sun dance during the celebration at Pine Ridge. They would sun dance in the morning, and then in the afternoon they would have the *wachípi* [dance]. They did it to bring our religion back to our people, and they were smart, because if they didn't start doing it, it wouldn't have come back. For the generation living now—the ones who believe in it and are walking with the pipe and everything—it would never have come back.

Who are these three men that influenced a whole generation? One was Frank Fools Crow, one was Grandpa Ben, and the other was Chris Big Eagle.[2] They are the three that coaxed a whole generation to come back to the Indian way, and I'm proud to have my Grandpa Ben with that. Even his sons and daughters did not know what he was doing. He saw a lot of things in his lifetime, and he knew it was going to affect later generations. He didn't want it to be lost because of what white churches had done to his people.

Grandpa Ben was sad at times. When I was small, I remember one time he was tanning hides outside. I was in about third grade. I remember this because Mrs. Lertz was my teacher at Pine Ridge. I came out of the house when he was tanning hides, and I asked, "Grandpa, how come you're so sad?" And he said, "Well, my people don't understand their way anymore. We want to bring back the Indian way. See, these things that we do here, it's good for our people by doing all this." For a young guy like me to hear my grandpa say this, it shocked me. It made me feel bad, and after that I sat up in the graveyard by Red Cloud's grave and wrote a poem for my class. I don't have it now.

The thing I remember most about my grandpa is what he said that day. Even when I was in high school, I used to think about it—about our ancestors, how hard they had it. They had to pray their way. And there I was sitting in the Catholic school, going to benediction every night, and I started realizing that these things were being forced on me. Forced onto me. I'm a Lakota, yet I didn't see these things of our people's ways. That's when I started picking up books and started reading. Then I went into the service and forgot all about it. I started drinking and doing drugs and stuff like that.

One day after I was back home and out of the service, my mom said, "You're ready." I turned and looked at her and asked, "What?" She said, "You're ready to go up on the hill." So I went to a man that I heard my grandpa say at one time could straighten out most of the older guys. A lot of them drank, and he had straightened them out. This was not a holy man. He's an *ikcéka wichášа*—a common man just like everybody else. A long time ago they were called *ikcéka wichášа*, but they were just as common as everybody else; they lived a common life. Then because of the visions they had, they were supposed to take that way of life. Thunkashila, the creator, gave them the vision to follow and to help the people.[3]

So I went to him, and he told me what I had to do—quit drinking, smoking dope and all that. He said, "Prepare yourself for one year to go up on the hill and pray and find out what you have to do to survive. Sometimes it doesn't take one year; sometimes it takes many years. It all depends. It might be for just one year."

And I prepared myself. I went up on the hill and prayed and came back down, and I found out I had to do it several more years. And the man said, "Well, this is your way of life. You have to keep going up. You're going to have to sun dance every year. Even if you don't dance, you must participate in the sun dance. Go; go help them with the rocks and the logs. That's all part of what you have to do. This is your way of life. This is what they wanted you to know a long time ago. That's why they gave you this understanding."

Going up on the hill got harder and harder. There are a lot of things that happened up there that I can't talk about. What happened up there was given to me, not to you or anybody. So I keep them in my heart and don't discuss it.

But it helped me to understand a lot of things about life and about people. I'd just sit there, and I could feel a lot of things. And feelings are one thing—emotions—that Lakotas thrive on. It's not how smart you are, but what you feel. When you feel here [in your heart], you understand how some other person feels, and you know that person and what they're all about. And if you know what they're thinking in their heart, and it's not the same as here [pointing to his head and to his heart], then there's a clash in your life.

ESTHER: I don't know why I told him it was time. I just went to him and told him it was time for him to do what he was supposed to do. And it's like he needed someone to tell him, so one day I said, "You'd better go down and get your pipe stem." Well, when he went down and cut it and brought it back—it was a long one, and he cut it in the middle—there was already a hole in it!

AARON: A natural hole in the pipe stem. After I carved it down and fixed it to fit the pipe bowl, it looked like there was a little eagle with the sun on it, and it looked like smoke was going back to the stem— all natural.

AARON: Before I got it, I prayed. Took me a half-hour to get it. I have all kinds of axes, chain saws and that, but I took a little butcher knife. The tree was ash, and it was so hard that it took me a long time to chop it down, but I didn't want to go back up to the house to get the axe, so I was sitting there with the knife and chopping it down.

They always say that the first pipe is the pipe that you make for yourself. When other pipes come, they're for the people. The first one you have is for yourself and for your family. When another one comes, it's the one that is used for the people. I didn't believe this when I got my first pipe, when I was going up on the hill. But later here comes another one, and another, and then here comes another one. The one that was the hardest to carry was the one that Chris [Sergel] gave back to the family. It didn't belong to my Grandma Lucy; it belonged to my great-grandpa.

AARON: I'll talk about the sun dance.[4] My grandfathers told me about the sun dance and how to do it, and I've been there and I understand what it is to live that old way. That means only the men danced in the sun dance. The women always danced underneath the shade among the people. They never did go in the center. The ceremony was for four days, and after four days they ended with a sweat. The sweat's for purifying before you go in.

There are many things that have changed in the sun dance over the years, because of individual understandings. My grandpas always told me that you should never change. You never add on, and you never take away. It's always the same. But over the years, they have added on, taken away, added on, and taken away, until it's completely different. Even the women go in the center and dance. And they have another tendency to change it too much by bringing horses in.

The sun dance in itself is a ceremony that is always straight and never goes backward. We learn from it; it's always good. I remember when dancers got up and went out there to dance. They danced for the people. Nowadays it's all getting out of hand—not only among the Indians. A lot of white people think that because they have gone to a sweat or to a sun dance, they know how to do it. They don't. So there's always somebody getting hurt. There were always secrets kept among the Lakotas about the way they do it.

Many of our ways people take and commercialize. I say my grandpas had to survive a long time ago, so they did things to survive. We don't have to do that now. We've got the freedom to pray our way and understand our way, so in order to understand our way, we have to respect what our grandpas had to do. We still have our warrior societies, veterans societies, and they're still all over the reservation. A lot of them are secret because of the other cultures intermixing with ours. The *akíchitas* are the ones in warrior societies and are the strongest.[5]

A man's strength lies in that pipe, in carrying the pipe for the family. The women never did do that. It was the men that carried the pipe for the family. But these things are changing. A lot of people are concerned about things, because there is turmoil in the sun dances all over. And it isn't one person's fault. Tunkashila (Wakhá Tháka) is trying to straighten it out. But many men don't have that understanding to carry on. Perhaps they understand, but they get confused and that causes confusion among the people.

HILDA: Are the people concerned? Are other young men concerned about how things are going?

AARON: A lot of them are concerned. Many are veterans that were in the war. They're really worried about it, and they want to cleanse their hands so they can go back out and help people.

HILDA: Do you take part in the sun dance?

AARON: Yes.

HILDA: The other day you said you began thinking about these things —the pipe and so forth—and it changed your life.

AARON: Oh, yeah, it really changed my life.

OLIVIA: When the eagles would come out of those cedars where we lived, even my husband—and he wasn't traditional—would say things about them. One day three little ones came out with the mother eagle and they were flying around above our place, and Hobart said, "Look over there." So I looked, and there was a big eagle flying around the little eagles. And this is what Hobart said: "Now you see, he wasn't aware of how the little ones were going to be flying, so he had to come out and check the mother out, to see how they were flying." "Now, that's just like us," he said, "We have to know that— how things are going with the children."

That was the story I told Aaron this morning. Even if his uncle, I said, wasn't traditional, he understood that part about the eagles.

AARON: A long time ago the Indians had all these values in the *thi-yóšpaye*. But their values came from watching the animals and the different things that were going on. And that's true. It's just like when

Auntie told that story about the eagles. That's a family. It's just like the deer, when they run in groups and the buck is always the protector, and they always watch the little ones. The bucks would take the orphans, and the orphans would run with the males all the time. A long time ago it was like that when Lakotas did things: the orphans ran with the warriors, the warrior societies. And the men who were orphans and didn't have fathers or grandfathers had to run with *tokala* [*thokála*] societies, the hawk societies. They didn't have a family, so they were there to give their life to the whole—to the people as a whole. The *tokalas* were always the most fierce in battle and the first ones to hunt for the people. They did not have families, so they did those things for the people.

Family values were established in them. But nowadays a lot of men who don't have their mom and dad go away from the reservation and end up living on skid row or something, and then they come back. They have lost their family values, and if they come back, they don't understand the Lakota ways, even though they are Lakota. The ways have to be re-taught to them, and it takes a long time and a lot of patience to do that, especially when they are older.

Today they don't take time to look at nature and understand it, like my Uncle Hobart did. This would be very simple, but they don't do that. Instead, they look at the white man's society and look at the dollar bills and the big houses and cars, and they want to get that way. But they don't have the knowledge to do that. White society's progress is on the outside; Indian society's progress is behind it. Even when the ones that are smart in our society go out into *wašíchu* society, they're low class. That makes them mad, so when they come back, they want to be big shots. Everybody thinks those people who came back are too much like the white man, so they're caught in the middle and are lost. All their knowledge has not been used.

What Auntie Olivia was talking about is the family values that are being lost because of the two different societies. Even a long time ago, the older ones used to think about it. Red Cloud wanted the Indians to be like the white man and to learn their ways, but they're having a hard time. The things that Lakotas usually wouldn't talk about, they do those things outside the reservation. And when Indians do it on the outside, if they come back, the people at home get mad at them, because it is wrong. But they did it that way on the outside to survive—a lot of our people do not understand that.

That's why there's such wide misuse of Indian religion and beliefs. People think they understand, but they don't. Nobody does, because out there they don't live the life that we live back here. We live our lives the Lakota way. When my mom was growing up, they lived their lives the Lakota way and their values were instilled in them. I can pick up a book and read about the white society out there, but I'll just have the knowledge—I won't have the understanding to live it because I haven't lived it myself. So that's the way it is outside the reservation. People can read a book—my grandfather's book or even this book—and they'll have the knowledge of it, but they won't know how to live it, because their life is different.

I've seen a lot of people who have read *Black Elk Speaks* or some other book, and they think they know everything. They say, "Why is it done *this* way? I've read about it being done *that* way." But always remember that the Indians don't give anything up. It's kept among the Indians. The people that come and tell us these things are white people—religious fanatics. We even had one get so mad that I had to tell him to leave. He believed he was one of the messengers that came down from the clouds to Great-Grandpa. You get that kind almost every other day, coming around and bothering you. That one man wouldn't leave us alone for about three months. He was from Omaha, but I forget his name.

ESTHER: He used to send letters and drawings to us.

AARON: Just because they read a book, they think they're experts in our way of life, but they're not, because they don't live it. We live it. I don't see those guys suffering for their people like we do. I see young men get pierced, and their pierce marks are dollar size. They suffer for all the people, and their prayers go out to all their relatives and all the Indian people. And then these guys [white men] come in and cut them down—say they don't know. But our young guys have been raised that way since they were small, brought up on our values.

I see white men come in and sit in one sweat, go back, and they're experts at it. Well, we've been sweating all our lives—one, two or three times a week. We live that life.[6] That way of life is coming back, and people want to be experts at it, to be knowledgeable about it, but they don't know how to live that life. There are a lot of feelings in the Lakota when he does these things, and outsiders don't understand. They haven't been raised on the reservation and lived the life that we do.

In fact, that attitude destroys the knowledge that we are trying to give them. They take a little knowledge and try to do our religious things out there, but they don't know what they're doing and they end up hurting people. You read about people dying in sweats and being left up on a hill. Those who do that do not know the responsibilities that we put on ourselves as pipe keepers for our people. When Lakotas do these things, they put their lives on the line to help the ones who need help. Those people on the outside don't realize that.

Another problem is that there are Indian people who are greedy, and so they want everything. There are Indian people—a lot of them—who charge for ceremonies. There's no way that our people back here can stop them from doing that because of the Freedom of Religion Act. A long time ago when they didn't have that act, our religion stayed on the reservation and didn't leave. Now they have the Freedom of Religion Act and the Indian people—the tribal governments—can't do anything to stop them.

The white churches—the Catholics and the Episcopalians and others—came on the reservation and those religions were forced on our parents, so they believe it now. But we are Lakotas, and we want to know our ways of life, and so we start living it. A lot of people who are strong Catholics ask us why we do that. "Why do you want to go back to that heathen way of life?" But it isn't heathen. We believe in the creator, too. We believe in the creation that's here. So do all religions—the Buddhists, the Catholics, and the Jews all do that same thing.

But that's the way it is. When the missionaries first came on the reservation, they wouldn't let the Indians practice their religion. They said they were the only ones that knew. "The only thing that's right is the Christian religion. We have to convert you. We have to save your life. What you're doing is devil worship." They didn't take the time to look at our beliefs. If they had done that, they would have seen that a lot of things were the same as theirs, a long time ago. But they didn't conform to what their Christian life was supposed to be like, as taught in the Bible.

They don't do what they're supposed to do. Instead, like the story in the Bible, Jesus went into the temple and coin collectors were there, so he threw them out. "This is my Father's house," he said, "we don't do that here." So he threw them all out, but after he threw them out, after he lived his life and died, they started doing it again. When you go to churches, they pass that basket along, and you put money into it. It's happening again—it didn't stop. I asked, "Why is that?"

LORI: What about the Native American Church?

AARON: Its principles are supposed to be based on all Indian religions, but today it's mostly peyote. Peyote is used in the religion of the Southwest Indians—that's the Navajo and the Hopis. In the Lakota religion, peyote is never used.

OLIVIA: We have Native American Church groups where I live. About four miles down the road, there's a clan there, a *thiyóšpaye,* and they're all Peyote. It's like a religion: they sing, and then they boil that stuff, and they drink it.

ESTHER: And the meetings, you know. It's their way of religion, I guess.

OLIVIA: Yeah, I attended one time, and I have a friend who belongs to one group. Her husband is the preacher, and they have the Bible. It's simply that they use peyote to drink like we do wine. And then they have a rattle and they sing their own songs. They have their own ceremonies. I really thought it was beautiful when I went. I mean, just the way they were singing, with that little rattle. But I didn't stay long, because then the preacher began talking about the religion part.[7]

The Catholic Church, mind you, at one time was so against the Indian religion that we couldn't even talk about our Indian religion.[8] But now, mind you, in church they're using sage, they're using sweet grass, and they're using the eagle feather. And they're using the pipe in church now. I shouldn't say this, but I haven't been to church. I'm part of a charismatic group. We have our own healing, and we have some people who even pray in Lakota with our healing. It really gets to you and when you believe, it happens.

That's the way we are now. The Indian religion's coming back; it's gradually coming back. We have it in the schools now. The schools are teaching Indian culture, telling about the Indian religion. Just the other day one of the ladies at Our Lady of Lourdes asked me if I would go and talk to the kids about the Indian religion. I told them I was too tied up with my work. But there is a big change going on now.

ESTHER: One time I got a call from a teacher at Red Cloud School. "Would you like to come over and talk to my class?" he asked. I said, "What kind of class?" And he said, "Theology." I said, "What do you want me to speak on?" And he said, "Indian religion. Do you think you can speak an hour?" I told him, "I don't know, but I'll try." He said, "If you can't, maybe you can bring something—a tape or something." I said, "All right, I'll do that." I had a tape—they all talked Indian on it, the Lakota language. So I took that tape to the school.

The teacher told the class, "Esther Black Elk DeSersa is going to speak on Indian religion and see if there is any similarity with the Catholic religion." I don't remember how many students were there, probably thirty or something like that. So I started out, "Our Lord, like the Indians, went up on the hill for four days, and our Lord fasted, too, up on the hill." So they asked questions and I'd answer, and I used the blackboard to illustrate. And then I said, "The sweat—they used to have something like a sauna, and the apostles used to go there. And the Indians had a sweat. It was not exactly alike, but there was a similarity." Then we talked about the cross. I drew a pipe from up on top—you know how it is, standing up? And then I said, "Now this is what my grandfather showed me. You see the cross on this side, and you see the pipe on this side, facing? He showed me on the ground: when you turn the pipe over this way, it makes a cross."

You know how children are; they just asked all kinds of questions. We went on and on, and all of a sudden there was the whistle—it was twelve o'clock noon. And I didn't even use the tape!

LORI: Aaron, I think you mentioned that some your age have moved away from the church. Are you connected with the Catholic Church still?

AARON: No.

LORI: Is that the trend for your generation, do you think?

AARON: When I started moving away from the church, there was one priest then who I thought was earnest about the religion. He was the only priest, and he has since retired and left as a priest. Then I started realizing that in the Catholic religion, even the priests retire. In our Indian way, Lakotas never retire. It was a lifelong thing, being a *wichášа wakhą́*—a holy man. They did it all of their lives.[9]

LORI: So when you're talking about the church and your traditions, you don't see a way of blending them very well?

AARON: There is a lot that is similar, that's good in both of the religions. It's what my Grandfather Ben always taught us: "Look and see. Whatever out there that is good, take the good and leave the bad."

But in order for the Indians to get their self-esteem back, we're going to have to learn the old ways, do things the old way, the way they were done before the European societies, the white societies, came in. Like in the old times, we have to get our strength back and understand what we're about in this world.

At the same time, there is a lot of interference by people out there who say they're healers but charge for their services. The Lakota doesn't. When one of our people becomes sick, or somebody is hurt, they freely give their help. But now people from the outside come to the reservation and take the healing out there and charge everybody. There's nothing they can give. They do not have the spirituality, the way of doctoring, the way of using medicines. They don't have any of that and they don't understand any of it. So when they try to heal out there, they hurt people. And that's what frustrates me.

It all started with the Catholic Church. And it's very hard on the youth now, my generation, because we grew up in a Catholic mission when they were supposed to integrate us into white society, and it was wrong what they did. You hear about these churches fighting for their religious freedom, but here they forced their ways on our people. And it isn't right. We never forced our ways on them. We think it's better if we keep our ways instead of forcing them on others. If they want to come and learn, we'll help, but we'll never give them anything of our ways. We always keep them to ourselves.

Our religious way is a way of life. It's not a church or an organization. It's the way we live and what we believe in our hearts. We never write anything down—no prayers are written down. The prayers from my great-grandfather that were said in that book came from his heart. When I go up on a hill, I say prayers that come from my heart. That's the way the Indians believe—our bible is this whole world. Everything is supposed to be sacred, but even among our people now it's being misused. It's misused because they see that almighty dollar. Instead of going out and working hard for what they want, like building houses or working as a secretary in an office, they go feed off our religious belief outside the reservation, because there are many people out there that want our spirituality. They go and they tell them things and they get money, and the people think they have spirituality. But they don't.

LORI: Esther, do you find it distressing to see your children leaving the Catholic Church?

ESTHER: You know, each individual is different. It's up to them what they want to do.

AARON: My dad was a strong believer in the Catholic religion. At one time, I was too, until I started seeing all these things. What pulled me to the Indian way was the realization that it never was forced on me: I went and walked it because I wanted to do those things. I wanted to say prayers to the Creator. It's like my grandpa said, "Many languages, you use many names, call it God, Creator, Tunkashila—it has many names."

I was afraid to pray for myself. Praying was for all the people, to help my people. Instead of taking up the Bible and reading prayers and learning from that and from mistakes, what I did was go back to our Lakota ways. I learned from our old people, sat down and talked to them about life long ago. They told me. If you're a good listener, you'll learn a lot. I sat with the old ones two or three hours, listening and not saying a word, while they talked. Now they're all gone, but what they said is in me. I'll always remember it, and that's what I have in me.

All my grandpas are gone. All my uncles are gone. So the knowledge is in me. And maybe when I get older, I in turn can tell the kids that are growing up. Because there are people older than me that are in their fifties and sixties, and they tell us, "We're the elders now. You have to respect what we say and do." I was taught to respect them and not to correct them, but they do things that are confusing the people. I see them going wrong, and I see confusion among my people about religious belief and understanding. But there's no way that I can go up to these older people and talk to them about it.

Maybe through this book that my mom and aunt suggested this will come out and things will be better. Right now the *akíchita,* the soldier society, is starting new. They're going to begin the old way of the sun dance next year. They're going to keep all the whites out, and they're not going to let women in the center. Those who bring people who don't belong to see the sun dance are going to be stopped at the gate. They're going to bring the old ways back. The *akíchita* were the ones that used to uphold the law of the pipe, and they settled disputes and provided security. They did all that, and that's what they're going to do now. So, in a sense, things are going back to the old way. If someone is doing something wrong, it's their job to correct it.

It's just like the Catholic Church. I look at the way it was a long time ago, when the apostles and priests used to go out and fast up on a hill, with no food or anything, and they prayed to their creator. They used to do all these things. They even used steam baths to cleanse themselves. But I see that they don't do that anymore, and now their structure is built on industrialization, like a nation and government. The Indian way was not like that. It was built on a way of life and what they believed. But the Catholics say, "Go to this church and pray, and all your sins will be forgiven by God." It's as if the Indians said, "Oh, if I go to the church, put five dollars in that basket that they pass around, then when all my sins are forgiven, I'll go home and just kick back and relax, you know." It's a lot easier to do that. It's simple. While the Indian way of life is harder and all year round.

When people come and want to have a sweat, we have to take them to the sweat and pray with them. And when you do that, you're giving your way of life. If something goes wrong in there, then everything will come back on you or on the person who runs that sweat or sun dance. That's why a lot of medicine men—spiritual leaders, they call themselves—get sick, because something's always going wrong. Sometimes they can't tell just what is wrong. The people are starting to hide things at sun dances, so the sun dance leaders start getting sick, and they go to the hospital with a heart attack or something. All those things are happening because people want to play with power. They want power.

HILDA: You have wonderful ideas, and you said your people are going back to learn the old ways. How should they live otherwise, how can they make a living?

AARON: They can go out and they can work for their money, go to school and get degrees. But that isn't enough, because it's an everyday, normal life.

When a Lakota starts his day, he prays, in the morning. When he ends it, he prays. That is almost gone now, but a lot of Lakotas still do that. The Lakotas say, "We can go pray any place, any time, anywhere. And your bible is in your heart; it's not where that church dictates."

HILDA: I should think that a lot of young people would be eager to join in with you.

AARON: They would, but the way society is right now, a lot of them are split. Many would like the power of the white man—money and influence.

HILDA: You were saying—I think you were saying—that white people are coming to some of your sacred places and putting on ceremonies, and you do not like that.

AARON: Yeah, they come in and just because an Indian takes them in and has them in a ceremony, and they learn songs and stuff like that, they think that they can do it and that they have authorization to do it. They don't. No man in this world can give that authorization.

The sun dance I used to go to was closed down this year by the Indians. I helped each year with things on the sun dance grounds. I built toilets and put them up. I then went out and suffered for my people out there. Most people are not interested in doing it that way. They are interested in paying a few dollars so they can sit there and say they were at a sun dance. Then they go back outside the reservation and say, "Well, I can do this." And so they create little gatherings all over, and then if something bad happens, they say, "The Indians taught me."

Some go up the hill—with pipes—and a lot of them are chased off the hill. If they get sick or something, they go back to their family and ask, "Why? Why is this happening? They said if I prayed with the pipe . . ." But they do not have a right to carry that pipe. Only certain people in the Lakota nation can carry a pipe. There's one out of the whole family who carries the pipe for the whole family. If a different person in the family had another vision that was strong, then the pipe would go to them.

In each family the pipe comes down, but there is never, ever a case in the Lakota nation where a woman carries the pipe. Only the male, the head of a family, does that. A woman never carries the pipe. Knowledge may skip a generation, and in that generation that it skips, it's the woman's place to watch over that pipe, but she cannot use it in ceremonies. She cannot take it out and use it. She just takes it and bundles it up and puts it away.

The pipe is only used for prayer, and it's not used to get what you want or for selfish reasons. It's like if I want a new car: I'll go out and work for it and buy it. You don't use the pipe to get material things. A lot of our young people want to learn it, but they go out and they travel all over, and then they come back to the reservation, and what they are looking for when they come back is power.

HILDA: What power?

AARON: Well, the young people think that Tunkashila will give them powers so that they can go up on a hill and pray and have a vision, and then have people flock to them. That ain't what it's all about.

Sooner or later, when we get too many material things—it happened to me twice in my lifetime, and I know. When I first started reading *Black Elk Speaks,* I had lost everything. I learned the hard way. I fell off once; I went and got drunk one night with my brothers and was sick for two weeks. Walking with the pipe is hard and you get frustrated, and you fall off. I know. I've walked with the pipe a long time. In order to live with a pipe and take care of it, there are a lot of things a man has to do to earn the right. And it's even more so for me, now that my great-grandpa's pipe is back in the house.

HILDA: Do you remember the time at a Neihardt Center spring conference when somebody asked me if my father "used" the pipe? I said, "Oh, no. Black Elk gave him the pipe, and he treasured it, but he just took care of it and did not use it." Then the man said, "Why not?" I answered, "He had too much respect. He respected it because Black Elk gave it to him, but he did not use it. He didn't ever use it."

AARON: When a Lakota gives a pipe to somebody, it's to complete something in his life. And when that's completed, the pipe always comes back to the family. If it went on through the next generation, then there's collaboration between families. Over the years, your dad [Neihardt] is gone, like my Grandpa Ben.

LORI: How do you feel about the fact that the pipe is at the museum at the Neihardt Center?

AARON: You mean, personally? It's up to them [gestures at Esther and Olivia] because they're the eldest in the family. They're the elders. That pipe was given to us for our understanding and to keep. As long as that pipe is there, and it's taken care of, and these things are continuing between Hilda's family and ours, it's all right.

HILDA: It's in a place of great respect. No one takes it out and puts on a ceremony or does anything with it.

AARON: But as soon as that friendship and everything ends, that's when the pipe will make its way back to the family.

HILDA: Well, that friendship is never going to end. No, it's just not going to end, because there are too many people coming along that care, really care.

AARON: That friendship can last for hundreds of years.

AARON: I told you about the sacred calf pipe that was given to our people a long time ago.

HILDA: I don't know which pipe you are talking about—the original one that the White Buffalo Woman brought to your people?

AARON: The original calf pipe. Everybody believes in that calf pipe, and all the ceremonies revolve around it—getting married, sun dance, sweat lodge. And the simplest interpretation of the Indian way is what gives us, the Lakotas, such power—enough to cure cancer. In all my days, I've been doing that, and I've seen four people cured of cancer.[10]

Elk's Head was the keeper of the sacred calf pipe—the original calf pipe. He didn't use that calf pipe. He cared for it. The descendants of the Elks are the ones who are supposed to keep the calf pipe. A long time ago when Indians were first put on the reservation, all these things were confiscated from the Indians. The Elks say the whites confiscated their pipe and shipped all these things to Washington. White Bull went to Green Grass to get that pipe and bring it back to Elk's Head, but it wasn't there. It could still be in the Smithsonian, hidden in the archives.

I've been to a lot of ceremonies, and in a ceremony they told me that the calf pipe was on a hill in a cave. So my brother and I thought it was in the Black Hills, and we were wondering about it. Then one day we were all sitting there talking about it—thinking about what we were told—that it was in a cave on top of a hill. Well, the Smithsonian is on a hill—Capitol Hill, you know—and the archives are like a cave underneath the ground. And all those articles and everything are in there. And that's where our family—the ones that do these things—feel the calf pipe is located, at the Smithsonian.

You know our belief shocks a lot of people.

My Grandpa Bill Horn Cloud told me he thought the pipe at Green Grass was not the calf pipe. Grandpa Bill Horn Cloud is Grandpa Ben's cousin. My Grandpa Bill was the main pipe maker; he made a lot of pipes for all these dancers—sun dancers all over the reservation. He made the pipes and he taught the art of how to make them. I had a lot of respect for him. Grandpa Bill, before he died, he said, "Well, I'm not going to be in this world long. I feel that I'm going to leave for the spirit world. I've never seen the calf pipe up there. I have never gone up there or anything, but I feel in my heart that the pipe kept there is not the calf pipe. I could be wrong, because I don't know. But I'm not going to be in this world very long, and that's the way I feel." A little later, he died.

Grandpa Bill said, "Your great-grandpa used to take and use that pipe." He even described it for me. The bowl was buffalo. Everybody thinks it's going to look like a buffalo, but it looks like a calf. If you look at a buffalo calf, it doesn't look like a full-grown buffalo. It's got a straight back, and thick legs. The stem is made out of wood, and there are twelve eagle feathers that hang from this stem. To identify it, there's a little round stone and seven circles on it. You have to know which way those seven circles are placed on the stone—that's the secret of it. Anyway, I'm not going to give that to you. The stone is with the pipe. It's what you call a pipe stone.

When you have that stone, you can see into the future. He had that strength. That's why my great-grandpa was a visionary—he could see into the future. He had that strength. But the interpretation is wrong. Even in that book that Raymond DeMallie put out, his interpretation is wrong—he tries to put him [Black Elk] in the spiritual sense only.[11] But if you look at it and try to understand what it is, it is the future of our people and what they hoped. Parts of it right now are passing.

HILDA: My dad thought it was real.

AARON: It's real life among our people. It's the *future* that your dad and grandpa saw. When you look at Great-Grandpa's vision, it's the future of our people.

LORI: You have talked about getting teachings from your Grandpa Bill Horn Cloud, but weren't there others, some other elders, who passed along their wisdom to you?

AARON: There was Grandpa Moses Runs Against.

ESTHER: He lived right north of Manderson.

AARON: He told us a story about how he had found this pipe that he carried all his life. It was sort of like mine—this long part and the stem. One day he was out digging postholes, and he hit a rock. He looked down in there, and dug around, and he pulled out a stone shaped like a pipe. It was white. He took it and brushed it off, and here it was—a pipe. He looked at it—there's the pipe and the hole was in there, so he just cleaned it out, all over, and then he went and made some kind of stem for it. He would take the pipe off the rack and show it to us, and say, "That's how things sometimes come." And he would also say, "A lot of times when the pipe comes, the stem is not with it. You get your own stem, put your own stem on it."

HILDA: May I ask you something? I have heard that you should not have the stem in the pipe all the time—that you're supposed to take it out. Is that correct?

AARON: Yeah, the stem and the bowl of the pipe are never put together unless you're using it. Just when you're going to use it—that's when you put tobacco in it.

OLIVIA: I never did take mine apart, ever since Papa gave it to me. I got it all wrapped up in the bottom of my trunk, together. That's the way he gave it to me, and that's the way it's been.

AARON: I and my brother Clif were at Grandpa Moses's house in the 1970s, just before the Longest Walk.[12] He said that before great-grandpa died, he told them that the religion that the Indians believe in was a good one and what he wanted. He said that he believed in that religion, and that's how he wanted to live his life. And not too long after that he died. My Uncle Hank, who was old and gray and half-blind, said, "I was there when he told us that, and he asked us to follow the Indian religion. I was too crazy to even try to pick up what I needed to do it. I couldn't pick it up. Now I'm sitting here. I'm old, and I'm still doing these foolish things. "But," he said, "maybe one of you, my nephews, would do it—bring it back to the family." He then gave us some yellow feathers, prayed over them, and gave them to us.

HILDA: Now we'd like to hear from you what you think is in the future.

AARON: Right now, we're going to what my great-grandpa describes in that book as the point where Indians all break off that road and go off on their own. The colors they use now on altars are all different. We never did use these colors. They had them, but they did not use them the way they do now. A lot of people say the four colors are the four races of man. But you know the four races on this earth. Great-Grandpa always told about it. There are the two-leggeds, the four-leggeds, the wingeds, and everything that grows on this earth. Those are the four people, and there's no color to them. There was no prophecy [of peace among all people]; there was no prejudice [in the idea of four colors].

HILDA: They [scholars and white people] just drag the idea in from the current problems in America and around the world . . .

AARON: They're judging people because of their color. That's all wrong. They're just seeing this world as being created by man himself. And it's going too far. That's why Great-Grandpa's vision shows us Indians getting distraught and going off that road. It shows little whirlwinds and heat, deserts drying up, and all that. That's all the storms and everything that's happening now—all the heat that you get in Arizona and the mud slides in California. Look at how many hurricanes hit the East Coast. That's all in the vision. Even the floods in the Missouri; it tells that when he comes to that river, he sees that man come out of that river that's causing all that flood.

ESTHER: The red man, red-blood river—

AARON: Yeah, that's what's causing all these floods. All those who live along the Missouri can get hurt because there's something wrong there. What they're doing is destroying Nature. When you build and move something, you always replace the amount that you removed. That way it keeps the world in balance. When you take something and start moving it around, something's always coming out of balance. And when something is destroyed on that land, something new should be put in place of it.

ESTHER: The simple explanation of that is when we go turnip hunting—when we dig turnips—we dig it out and take the turnip parts, and then we take the top and put it back in place, in that hole.

AARON: Yeah, and then new turnips grow. What you take out you put back in, and so it grows. If you destroy a tree by cutting it down, every tree that you cut down, you replant, putting a tree there so it grows. But when they started destroying the trees and not replacing them, because they're making fields out of it or something like that, that's wrong. It's causing this whole world to come unbalanced.

It's just like the cherries. Cherries—a long time ago they used to say "they pout." Once all these people came along and they cleaned out all the cherry trees on this side of the fence by the road to put in a telephone line. For four years the cherry trees on the other side didn't give any fruit. They pouted, and they didn't give you their fruit for another four years. When you destroy something of theirs, they won't give the fruit to you.

It's just like when they get a tree for a sun dance and cut it down. They're taking a life, and the spirit of that tree takes their prayers to Tunkashila. They always offer something. They give it food and everything when they dig that center hole. They put *wasná*, choke cherry juice, tobacco, everything down that hole. Then they put that tree in there, and the spirit of that tree has that food to take it to the spirit world. So—see—that's all there.

But nothing is replaced now, so Nature is always trying to balance itself naturally. By doing what people do, it takes life. It kills people. It kills trees. The birds are killed, the deer and all four-leggeds. It even kills us two-leggeds. And everybody's asking why. They should stop and think why. Man is not as natural as an animal, and animals are trying to tell man what went wrong, but he won't listen. Now they're starting to get diseased because of what man has done. Even man's domesticated animals are getting diseases—they've got disease in meat.

It's just like describing the four directions on the Sacred Hoop. Everybody misinterprets. They say four directions, but it's called four winds—*thatúye tópa*. For the west, they use black and blue; they use the colors. The west means darkness and the water that comes with rain. It can destroy, and it can also make life. The Indians pray for life, and they ask, and rain is sent from the west. The clouds start coming, and you get rain and showers and it makes things grow. But it also carries a disruptive power. It destroys things that are not right— things that are not good for this world. And when you pray, you have to realize that these things are there and how you can control it, to understand that Tunkashila gives Indians life and how to bring it without destruction.

White is in the north, but it isn't really white; it's a cleansing power. And what comes from the north? The snow, and that time when the snow and winter come, it comes and cleanses everything around us.

The Indians never did hunt rabbits until after the first heavy snow. It kills all the germs. There are a lot of rabbits that have a disease, and it kills all that. Rabbits are only hunted in the wintertime.

For the east, they say red, and they associate it with the sun, the rising of the morning sun, the daybreak star. That's where that knowledge comes from. The Creator's like a light, and the knowledge is there.

The ones that carry the *hóchoka* [sun dance tree] are the ones that carry that pipe.[13] One of them carries the stone that took care of the calf pipe, and they're the ones that help the people. People don't realize that only a few are picked, and they seldom talk about it. My great-grandfather was one of them, and the knowledge was passed on. He didn't want to die and leave the knowledge unlearned, misunderstood.

There are many times that I have gone to Green Grass and I talked about our religious ways, and even if the pipe kept there is not the real calf pipe, it's our way of life that is in that pipe, in our prayers. I know it's being heard, and the simplest interpretation of the Indian way is what gives us, the Lakotas, such power. I have seen a lot of things happen. I've seen women cured of cancer at the sun dance—the cancer taken out of them. And I saw it fool doctors, because when the women went back to their doctor, the cancer was gone. The doctors didn't understand how it was gone, who had the knowledge to do that. I've seen miracles happen, things happen in life when a prayer was given. And I've seen life taken because of misuse of it, too.

Many people think it's just the prayers that cure, but the Indians have medicine they don't tell anybody about, which they use when people get ill. They still use the medicine, and at the sun dances they have it and make it. They don't tell them how they mix it. After they take people out in the sun and pray for them, they bring them back and give them their medicine and the sickness is gone. The old-time medicines are still here, and there are a lot of young people who know about this medicine. They don't talk about it, because it belongs to the Indian people. It can help many people, but the people on the outside have a tendency to misuse it.

It's just like my great-grandpa's book: people are walking on this road and some go off the road. As I've said, my great-grandpa's vision wasn't a spiritual vision. It was the future of our people, the Lakota people. Some people don't look at it that way—they want it to be spiritual and have a deep meaning. But what it is, when you look at it and interpret it, is what our people are going through in this life and in the future, and how they're going to be put back on that good road—bringing back the old ways and ceremonies and understanding them.

Many Paths

HILDA: Can you tell something about preparing for the sun dance?
OLIVIA: They choose a tree and cut it down and bring it in to the place of the sun dance. And the girl that comes along when they bring it in has to be a virgin. They sing as they bring it in, and they come in on the east side of the dance place, and they set it up. Sun dancers make flags—red, blue, white, and yellow—using about a half-yard of material for each color. Then the sun dancers put the flags on the tree before they put the tree up. Next the sun dancers make tobacco ties. They make so many for each dancer, and all this is for healing. Each one that dances commits himself to somebody that he is dancing for—someone who is sick or bedridden. Then they tie all the tobacco ties on the tree, and then the ropes or thongs are tied on, and then they start piercing.[1]
LORI: What is the meaning of the sun dance?
ESTHER: The sun dance is a religion where they had to suffer, and they pierced just like our Lord was pierced. There's a similarity there.

At one time the Catholic Church did not want the sun dance religion, so the Indians had to hide and have their own sun dance. I remember going to Spring Creek on Rosebud. I was small. I went in a wagon. I don't know, but I think it took two days to get there. We went with our grandfather, and that's something I can always remember. I thought it took days and days to get there in the wagon, and I remember a lot of people and wagons.
OLIVIA: The people who are going back to the traditional sun dance —well, there is a lot of meaning to it, just like Aaron explained, but there are also people who want to show the white people what it's

like to have a sun dance. So there is one sun dance down there that the white people can go to. And you wouldn't believe it, but there are some white people doing the sun dance. It's at Fools Crow, in Kyle, right below the college center. Why would we keep it a secret and not let the white people in? The reason for that sun dance, from the way I understood it, is that no matter what color we are, we're supposed to unite and stand together. Reconciliation is what I'm trying to say. Let them know because they want to know. They want to be a part of it. There are many Indian people on the reservation that are married to white people, and those white guys all want to participate, but they can't do it.

HILDA: That's Indian women married to white men? And they won't let the white men take part?

OLIVIA: No, and there're Indian boys married to white girls. I have a grandson that's married to a white girl, and she acts more Indian than my kids! She really learned lots, you know.

HILDA: Well, a lot of the white people are sincere in respecting you and these ceremonies. There are some for whom it's a kind of sentimental notion, but many are truly sincere. The spiritual ideas that came from your grandfather have inspired many people all around the world. But apparently Aaron feels this way—"Stay away and let us have our religion."

OLIVIA: Yeah, that's the idea that he is giving us. I work with a lot of people, and I see a lot of people, and I'm good to them, and they're good to me. I don't say, "No, you can't do this, because you're different." I'm not that type of person. I always tell my kids, "I don't care where you go or what you do, you want always to help somebody who needs help, because in the Bible it says that when you help and when you give and share, you get it back double-fold." And that's how I feel.

HILDA: Do you think more Indian people—more Lakotas—feel the way Aaron does or the way you do?

OLIVIA: They feel like they want to keep it for themselves and not share that feeling with another person. I don't know why.

HILDA: You can understand that feeling, though. They want something that belongs to them alone.

OLIVIA: It belongs to them. I know it belongs to them, but still it's a religion, and we should learn to share. We should share, really.

HILDA: You know, Black Elk said, "If the vision was true and mighty then, it is true and mighty still, and it is for all people." He wanted it to go around the world, which it has. But I do understand how Aaron and the other Indian people feel. I understand that very well. Do you think more people feel the way Aaron does?

OLIVIA: Yeah, I know that. Like this sweat lodge—years ago when they went into the sweat lodge, it was to purify one's self and get ready for the sun dance. But now that purification through the sweat lodge is for anybody who goes in there. And I don't know if they get the feeling of it. Of course, myself, I've never been in a sweat lodge, so I don't know the experience of it.

ESTHER: Since Grandpa became a catechist, in talking to him, he would say the religion is similar to the Indian religion. I asked him, "What do you mean?" And he said, "We all believe in one person. But what's the difference? No matter where you pray—even in the hills, or even here, or in church, it's all the same." So he used his pipe in the morning—evenings, too. And still he prayed with the rosary; so he believed in both. Well, there is a similarity. He would fast. It was on a mountain. He fasted on a hill. Well, the Indians fasted on a hill, too, for four days. These are all similarities.

To me there is a similarity between the Catholic and the Lakota religions. So I go to church when I want to. And then sometimes I don't go, but I still pray, even when I'm outside. Sometimes I take walks and I pray. No matter where you pray, it's the same.

OLIVIA: The Lord hears you.

AARON: Mom would say, "Well, I want to go to church for Easter." And everybody was sitting around, thinking about it, and I said, "Well," and all of us boys would look at each other, "Well, shall we go to church? Might as well, might make it storm!"

ESTHER: I think it's up to the individual. I even went to church because my friends wanted me to go, and I went to different churches. You have to find out what's going on, what's the difference.

OLIVIA: Religion was forced on us in school. Now I feel good about how I pray, and I'm really close to the Lord now, more than ever before. I never depended on the Lord [before]. My life style was here and there, you know, a thing I did from day to day, and I never depended on the Lord. Now I do; now I'm with the Lord. I'm praying all the time—praying for my kids, praying for everybody, praying for the sick. We do healing at my house; so it's different now in my life.

These people are talking about the Indian religion. I believe in it; I was raised with it. I have a lot of respect for it, but I still have my own religion.

HILDA: You don't practice it?

OLIVIA: I don't practice it. That's the difference between us.

LORI: And yet, you have this Black Elk Museum in your home, which is dedicated to your grandfather, your father, and the teachings of the Indian religion.

OLIVIA: Yes, I do, and the biggest thing I am trying to do is to build up the Black Elk Museum.

LORI: What about the ancient religion, the Indian religion?

ESTHER: That's coming back. A lot of the younger ones are talking about spirituality—the Indian religion. It's coming back more than ever since after the [Wounded Knee] occupation, isn't it?

CLIFTON: Lots of them are sun dancing.

ESTHER: We're all interested in Indian religion—everybody, but—

CLIFTON: Everybody's so modernized nowadays. You're interested in it, but you still have to live the way you've been raised. You've got to make a living. You can't go back to the way people used to—to the old days—because you could never do it. A lot of them talk about it, but they can never do it.

LORI: Are people finding a way to incorporate some of the ways of the old religion without going back, or is that hard to do?

ESTHER: Some people talk about religion, and then there're some people who make it up the way they want it. It's like the sun dances. There was always one way they used to do it years ago, but after that, some start sun dancing here, and they make up what they're supposed to be doing. They add on and they leave things out. They're falling away from the traditional one. They just do what they want to.

CLIFTON: It's like you go from one sun dance to another sun dance. They do it different from the other one. It's just like going to different churches. They've got so many sun dances going on now, more than there are powwows in the summertime. And they're saying now that the sun dances and the powwows are competing against each other. People go to one sun dance, and then they don't believe in the other sun dance over here—they say they are doing it wrong. I've been to a couple sun dances; you always hear somebody talking that way. It's like you've got all the Catholic Churches and different churches, and you don't know which one to believe. That's the same way with some of the sun dances now. You don't know which one to go to, which one to follow or believe in.

HILDA: Does the sun dance take the place for a lot of people of going to church or believing the pipe religion? Does it take the part of a religion in their lives?

CLIFTON: Not really, because I know a lot of people that sun danced and everything before, but they go to church every Sunday, too.

ESTHER: So they go to them both. We pray to the same Creator.

HILDA: Have you been to a *yuwípi* ceremony?[2]

ESTHER: Yes.

HILDA: Could you tell us about it? My father wanted your grandfather to do a *yuwípi* ceremony, but he said he didn't want to do it.

ESTHER: Well, my grandfather didn't do *yuwípi*. He said it was different. I suppose they healed, too, in it—different ones, different ways. I know my grandfather healed in the daytime and at night with the lights on.

OLIVIA: I went to one, and I swear to God I'll never go to another one. That one I went to was for my aunt; she had cancer of the throat. She knew they couldn't do anything about it, but she still wanted to go to the *yuwípi*. So we went, and it was real dark, and they started to sing. The person doing the *yuwípi* talked in Lakota, and they [the spirits] talked to him. We couldn't hear them talking to him, but he answered them. And when he was asking, that person doing the *yuwípi* was all wrapped up in the middle of the floor. I had my glasses on, and they told me to take off everything—my rings and glasses. And after that, that rattle traveled all over in the room and little sparks came out. And this thing came and hit me right on the feet, just kept hitting me. Pretty soon it was hitting me at the head—kind of hit my glasses, so I took my glasses off and put them on my lap. And it kept after my feet, because we all sat like this, with our feet out in front, so it kept bouncing on my feet.

I thought, "My goodness, what's going on here?" So finally I thought I'd better start praying. But I was kind of scared—you know how it is when it's dark and all that. I said, "Please, Lord, don't let it do that to me," and I panicked. It finally left me when I did start praying.

When they turned the lights on, that blanket that the person doing the *yuwípi* had on was folded up real nice. I couldn't figure that out. So after it was over, I told the man, the one having the *yuwípi,* "I'm never going to come to *yuwípi* anymore. That scared me out." And he laughed.

HILDA: Esther, when you went, was it the same time, or another time?

ESTHER: It was another time. My niece came over and said, "I'm going to this ceremony at Porcupine. Do you want to come with me?" So I said, "Okay." She called this one person and told them, "My aunt is coming with me." I had a meeting that evening, but in the meantime they had cancelled the meeting, so I went. Aaron and I went with her, and we had one little girl with us.

AARON: They were helping this one woman; she had arthritis and everything. We were praying for her; so all those people who went to the ceremony to pray for help prayed for her and everything that they needed help for, too. So that's why we went to the *yuwípi* ceremony.

ESTHER: It was in a basement of a house. We went in, and they closed it, and it was pitch dark. So we were sitting there on the floor in a circle in the basement. A lot of people were in there. You can't wear shiny things; I had to take my glasses off. When they started, you could see sparks. And this rattle went all around and hit this one boy. You could just tell it hit. You know how it sounds when it hits a person's head. And then it continued rattling, but it never did come to us in the corner.

I was sitting there, and my niece told me what she wanted. Pretty soon they started telling—different people got up and told what they were praying for, for somebody to get well or things like that, and then they'd say, *mitákuye oyás'į* [for all my relatives].[3] Everybody was afraid of it, I think, going down the line. One person started praying, and then the next one in the dark. Then it came to me, and I heard some rustle, but I didn't say anything. I heard this voice saying, in Lakota, "Your niece is not going to say anything. When you pray, you tell him what your niece wants." That's all it said. I don't know if it was my grandfather, or who it was, but it was an old man's voice.

So I prayed for whatever she wanted—that she'd lead a good life and things like that. I prayed that way. And I listened to see if she would say anything, because this person told [me] she's not going to say anything. And then it went on to the little girl, and all she said was *mitákuye oyás'į*. We taught her how to say it. So when it came to my niece, I listened, and all she said was *mitákuye oyás'į*. She didn't say anything. And then it went to Aaron, and he sounded like an old man talking. Pretty soon, he came back to his own voice. And then this one person that was sitting over there, I think he had some problems—that rattle hit him a lot of times. I don't know what the message was there. Nobody was wrapped up; this was a thanksgiving ceremony, a *wóphila*. Anyway, we were sitting there, and this rattle never did come to us, in the corner where we sat.

And then the light came on afterward. It was interesting. I couldn't get over it. I told my niece what I had heard. This voice I heard was an old man's voice, but it made me think it was my grandfather. And so when we came out, there was thunder and lightning all the way around, and right in the middle you could see the stars. We got home to the house, and we all got out, and we looked up again, and it was still there—the thunder and lightning all the way around, but in the middle were stars.

I've gone to other *yuwípi* ceremonies. I remember one time I went to one at Grandpa Big Road's house. My mother had lost her wedding ring, and she was worried about it. So I remember going with my mother and dad, and we went there, and it was light at that time. They had the ceremony and then it was evening. I remember Big Road said, "Go back and look under the wagon tongue." So we came home and looked under the wagon tongue, and it was lying right there. We usually camped out. We washed in a basin a lot. The ring must have fallen in there, and she had thrown it out. So they found her ring for her!

At one time in a ceremony someone didn't believe in *yuwípi.* They just went along with it and sat there. But the holy man knew, and he said, "Someone in here doesn't believe. Light the lamps. Light the lamps." They were all looking at her, and a pile of sage was on her head. She did not feel it, but they were looking at her head. She reached and felt the sage.

Strange things happen, sometimes.

Lakota Legends and Stories

This would be a good time to repeat a story that Lucy, Black Elk's daughter, told me and that I recorded on 30 March 1977, when she was visiting at my home in Columbia, Missouri. Here is how it went.

LUCY: Once upon a time in the olden days, the Sioux Indians had a lot of stories about the *iktómi,* who were like the jokers we now have everywhere.[1] But the one the Indians told about was Iktómi, who was also a joker. Now we call him a joker, but he is an *iktómi,* and he does a lot of good deeds for the people. But sometimes he fools them; he does wrong things with the people. So that's how come they call him a joker—*iktómi,* which means spider. I don't know if he's named after the regular spiders now. He's a person, you see.

So this camp—there was a camp—the people were camping on one side of the creek. This Iktómi was going along the creek or river, and he ran into something that was just breathing so hard, like there was a wind blowing dust. And Iktómi approached this thing. He would wake him up; he was sleeping. It was a *big* giant. At that time they called it the *íya. Íya* means you've got a big mouth and can eat up anything—people and anything. So it was kind of a creature lying there.

And pretty soon this Iktómi went close to this creature. The *íya* woke up, and it kind of took a big breath and just kind of blew the *iktómi* over. And so Iktómi says, "Who are you?" And he says, "I'm called Íya, or giant, that would eat anything like human beings or anything." So this Iktómi—in the Indian way he kind of got mad at him when he blew him over—said, "Why, you know you haven't got much in you. You know I could do this." Iktómi said that. And this *íya* got kind of scared, and he said, "Well, this is where I live; the giants live here."

And then Iktómi said, "You're my brother. When I first created the creatures, I made something like you. I created you." [Lucy laughed at that.] "And now we're both brothers, and there's a bunch of people in the camp—*big* camp—real fat ones." Iktómi was the one who said it, and he said, "I think you and I should invade that camp, and we can have a real big dinner," he says. "They're so fat."

"But I'm gonna ask—what are you scared of?" he said to Íya, this giant. The giant said, "I'm scared of people hollering—hollering and screaming and beating on a drum."

And Iktómi said, "That's just what I am scared of." So he said, "You're my brother. Sure enough, you're my brother. It happens I'm scared of drums, too, *pounding.*"

And then he said, "I'll see which side of the camp you're gonna come on and which side I will come on. We're going to go half-and-half," he says, "so I'll go into camp and find out." And so he went into the camp, and he just ran, ran along the camp in a circle. And he said to the people in the camp, "There's a big giant called Íya lying by the creek, and I tell you, I'm going to come and bring him along. He says he's scared of hollering people, screaming people, and drum beating. So when we show up, you all holler and beat the drums."

So Iktómi went back and said, "Everything is all right. Now, you go on this side, and I'll go on the other." Íya made *such* a noise, but when they were getting closer, why the people hollered and they beat drums, and they were screaming, so Íya just went in and toppled over—*dead.*

Finally Iktómi said, "You go on." And Iktómi turned, and he cut Íya open—he cut his belly open, and here came out a bunch of people—riders, travois, and all kinds of people—children and everything. Last of all came a covered wagon. I think it was those persons in that fight called The Hundred Slain—that fight where the hundred persons were killed. And then came the Indians. They were still on foot, and they were walking up. And then came our agent—he came up!

That was the *íya*—out of the belly of Íya!

LORI: We would like for you to tell some of the stories, about birds and so forth, which your father or your grandfather told you.

ESTHER: Oh, I know one. Do you remember the dance in the circle? Iktómi came along when they were having a dance and told them to dance in a circle with their eyes closed.

OLIVIA: —so all the while they were dancing with their eyes closed, Iktómi was digging up the food that they had in the ground there. They were cooking it. So Iktómi took all their food. Then one of the people opened his eyes and saw that the food was all gone, and he said, "They fooled us again!"

My father told us that the moral of this story is that we should keep our eyes open so that we could not be tricked.

ESTHER: That was another story. In this one, prairie chickens were having a dance—dancing in a ring. This really happens; they dance in a circle. The prairie chickens were dancing, and there was one for security on each of the four corners, and they heard this Iktómi come along. He told them to keep on dancing and to keep their eyes closed. They were dancing, and pretty soon Iktómi was clubbing them on the heads—killing them. The prairie chicken guards hollered, "Run! Go home! They are killing us!"

This is kind of a fairy tale, and it means that people are going around killing animals, just for their feathers or for their hides.

HILDA: The other day you mentioned something about the rabbit dance and how it began. Can you tell us that now?

ESTHER: That's a kind of a fairy tale. Two men were hunting. They were tired, so they lay down to rest with their heads on the ground, like they were sunning themselves. Soon they heard a thumping noise, so they crawled up a hill. The noise was two rabbits going around in a circle and dancing. The rabbits flapped their feet on the ground, and it sounded like a drum beat, and they were going along like they were dancing.

And one man said, "Look at them; they keep time when they go." And the other one said, "And their feet sound like a drum beat." So they kept on watching it, and pretty soon the first one said, "Do you know what we'll call it? The rabbit dance." So one of these men started singing a song, and that's how the rabbit dance came about—from watching those two rabbits.

OLIVIA: Grandfather used to tell us stories. They were what you would call legends. I always remember this one little story that he used to tell us. The birds had all gathered, and they were having a competition. And the birds said, "Who can fly longest up in the sky?" So then they all flew now, and one by one the birds were falling; they couldn't take it. Then here came the eagle—the almighty eagle—and the eagle flew and flew and *flew*. He finally came down, and they said he was the winner.

But no—somebody spotted a little bird up there. So they watched that little bird, and he flew around and around, and finally he came down. It was a little hummingbird, and so they asked the humming-bird, "How did you do that? How did you stay up there so long?" So the little hummingbird said, "Well, because I rode on the back of the eagle." I thought that was real cute.

The meaning of the story, as it was told to us, was that we have to use our heads to do things. We have to use our minds. And the little hummingbird used his mind and rode on that eagle, so he didn't have to fly all the time and get played out.

ESTHER: And the other meaning—this little hummingbird couldn't tell a lie. You shouldn't tell a lie. They all had meanings, all those stories. Olivia told that story, but we all know about it. It's just like teaching children not to lie: this little hummingbird didn't lie, because he told the truth—that he was on the eagle's back. That's what teaches these children not to lie.

OLIVIA: I know another one. There was a fire and a bean and a stick, walking down the road. They came to a creek, and so they were try-ing to figure out how they were going to go across. So then the stick said, "Well, I'll lie across the creek, and the bean can walk over me, and then the fire can walk over me." So he lay down across the creek, and so the little bean started to walk across, and then the fire came. And as the fire came, he just burned that stick up, and then finally they both fell in the creek, and then the fire went out. So the little bean got a big kick out of it, and he just laughed and laughed. Pretty soon he burst!

The moral to the story is—the way it struck me—was that they were trying to use their heads. Now when they did, the little bean walked across the stick and then the fire went and burned the stick up. Then the stick fell in, and there was nothing but the little bean, and he thought that was funny and he just laughed and laughed. And then they found that the little bean had popped open.

ESTHER: But there was more to the moral. They never survived, and you should think twice, instead of doing it right away. The main thing is that you have to think before you act.

OLIVIA: Now I tell those [last] two stories to my grandchildren, just the way that Grandfather told them to us.

ESTHER: Sometimes I have my grandchildren over at my place. And one night I lined them all up. I put a blanket on the floor, and I lined them all up on the floor and they said, "Tell us stories. Tell us stories."

And I lined them up, the biggest down to the littlest, and I was telling them stories. They were all just sitting there. "If I tell you stories, you're going to have to tell me stories. But you can make them up."

I kept on telling them stories. "Another one," they said. "No, it's your turn to tell the stories," I said.

So every one of them, the older ones, told stories—nursery stories, like "The Three Bears." And it came to the little ones, and I said to my grandson Sherman Jr., "What about you? Are you going to tell me something?" He said, "Well, I don't know stories."

I said, "Oh, they all told stories. What are you going to do?" He said, "Well, I don't know . . ." I said, "Do you want me to skip over you?" "No! No! No!" And so he sat up, "You know, Grandma, I'm so sleepy I can't keep my eyes open." I said, "Do you want to go to sleep?" "No," Sherman replied, "No, that's what I want to tell you. That's how some little puppy died."

They can have an imagination, too. He was sleepy, and yet he just came out and said, "That's how the puppy died."

Women and Men/Men and Women

Women and men/men and women is a most interesting and at times controversial topic among the Lakotas. We talked about that a bit, and it was soon apparent that women's rights are bringing with them growing pains, not just in the white world, but in both societies.

ESTHER: Long ago, when they were courting, the man would usually go to the parents and ask for the hand of the lady.[1]

OLIVIA: The young man would have to take horses or whatever he had for the bride, for the lady. It's a gift that he gave for her, because he liked that girl. He wanted to marry her.

AARON: I'll explain it in modern days. If somebody's going to marry your daughter, you look at them and make sure they love each other and everything, but also you look at the son-in-law and see if he can provide for that family and take care of it. A long time ago, it was really the same thing. When they gave gifts to the Indian parents, like horses and hides and all that stuff, they were showing the parents that that young man could provide for a family, and he had great honors in the war. That was what he was showing them, so he could get the hand of their daughter.

When the courtship was over—my Grandpa Horn Cloud told me one day—you bring them to get married, and they would bring a shawl and put it around both of them. And the medicine man or spiritual leader would come up with the pipe and they'd make their vows with that pipe and a prayer, and the young man would carry the pipe. The vows were made with that pipe so they could stay together.

HILDA: Do you and Esther know about marriages in the old times, before the church ceremonies?

OLIVIA: In the olden days? They got married through ceremonies. In June of 1995 I went to a wedding ceremony that was like a traditional one. They did it way out there in Whirlwind Horse's, in the buffalo pasture, right on the reservation. It was the prettiest place you ever saw—all the pine trees and the sun dance grounds are way down in there. It's all open, and there are trees around. The tents were all inside of those trees, camped there. They had this marriage ceremony after the sun dance. I got invited because I did quilts for the lady that was going to have that give-away after the ceremony.

The girl rode a horse with her beaded Indian outfit on, and the boy stood up there on the hill, where they were going to get married. There was a pine shade there. She rode up the hill, and the spiritual leader took the girl by the hand and took her over to this guy. Then he had the ceremony with the pipe. He had the pipe and cradled the pipe to the four directions. And then he took sage—either sage or cedar. Boy! It smelled good! He just went around with that sage and came in and said more prayers. Then he gave them a bowl—it had cherry juice and that *wasná*—and they drank. Everything was said in Indian, in Lakota.

What I understood him saying is that they were put together and that they should have a good marriage. They were the ones responsible for the children, and should give good examples to the children. And they should raise the children right, and not just be good to one another. That's the way I understood him in Lakota. That's what he said.

Oh, the couple was dressed pretty. They wore identical clothes. They had ribbon shirts, and he had a pair of black pants on and she had a black skirt on with a ribbon shirt matching. Someone had made them a trailing star quilt; it was a broken star, and they held it together on them. He held it here [touches one shoulder] and she held it on the other side, on their shoulders. And they went around the arena and the drummers sang an honoring song. Like a little flower girl, two boys and two little girls held that quilt up like this. Her folks and his folks walked behind them, and then everybody followed. They all went around there. And I thought that was beautiful.

Now, I don't know if they were married in the eyes of the law or in the eyes of God, but they were married in the eyes of the pipe and the people. Yes, I know that in the eyes of the people, they were married.

HILDA: In the old-time ceremonies, then, the people would be there so everybody would know?

OLIVIA: Everybody. They didn't just say, well he performed a marriage right here. How would the people know that? They did it out where there was a crowd.

And then they had the biggest feast after that. You should have seen the watermelon—they had two truckloads. And, oh, they had lots to eat!

AARON: Now my Grandpa Bill said, "Indians had divorces, too." When they couldn't get along, couldn't be together any more, they'd bring that same pipe, and that medicine man would pull that pipe apart, and they'd go their separate ways.

ESTHER: Now when they do that, when there's a divorce—the Lakota way—they beat their drum. They call it *bubúhigla*—and they beat that drum as hard as they can beat it, and they all come around, and then that's when they return the pipe and pull it apart.

HILDA: If they lived in a home together, what happened to all the possessions? Did they go to the wife? What happened to the tipi and all the blankets and everything?

AARON: It would go to the people. When they divorced, the woman would move back in with her family, and the man would go back to his family, and everything that they had—

ESTHER: They gave it to the needy.

AARON: The needy. But then they had another tradition, too. Instead of one wife, they used to have three or four wives. They married sisters; if they married one, they married the other sisters in the family.

ESTHER: The men have their own responsibilities, and the women have theirs. And even when they have a feast, all the women sit on one side, and all the men on the other side, and the children take their plates over to them. And even in the Catholic Church, a long time ago, all the women sat on one side and the men on the other side. That's the way things were years ago.

They did things separately. The women took care of the children, making their clothing, or whatever, and cooking things. Then there're the men—they were the hunters and protected the family. All the men came together for a council meeting, all the ones who came from each *thiyóšpaye*. But it's altogether different now; women are involved in it.

AARON: A long time ago when they went to ceremonies, the men would come into the kitchen and eat. The women would all go into the living room and visit, and the men would talk together. And in the Lakota way of life, it was like that. The men were always the hunters. The women didn't go out and hunt; the men did. And the women were always the ones that pitched the tipis. Nowadays the men are putting up the tipis, because many women don't know how.

One time we went to the Crow Fair, and none of us knew how to put up a tipi, so my mom had to show us. That's what I mean: the younger women nowadays are relying too much on the white man's society to understand true Lakota traditions. They're getting into the sun dance and they say, "We don't have any husband to take care of us." That's why the societies were there in the old times. They could go to these people in the societies for help, and those people would help them.

Nowadays because of the aspects of the white man's society that have come in, our traditions are being turned topsy-turvy. A lot of the women are doing what the men are supposed to do. It's hurting our society. It's even hurting our ceremonies. Women are telling the men what to do in their ceremonies, and it's not supposed to be that way.[2]

AARON: A long time ago, the Creator gave the calf pipe to the men to take care of for the nation, to lead the nation and to walk with it. And they gave a gift to the women of the nation. They were given the right to cleanse themselves and also to give birth to the nation

The strengths are equal. When those two strengths come together, they clash, and they can hurt the people. So the men keep this over here and the women keep that over there. The time of cleansing and giving birth is hers, and the women always took care of that. The men took care of the suffering and the protection and feeding of the people. For that they formed societies like the *tokala* and the different *akíchita* societies. The pipe and the ceremonies and the sun dance were all done by the men. One ceremony among the seven was given to the women: that was when a girl became a woman. Then that ceremony is done, but the other ceremonies were given to the men.

The men have to suffer in the sun dance, because the women suffer to make the nation. A long time ago when they had sun dances, the women never were inside the circle. The men were in there suffering for the people. The women never did go in there because of the clash. Nowadays a lot of them go in the circle, and people get hurt or sick over it. It's even taking a toll on the sun dance leaders. Many of them have heart attacks and stuff like that.

A long time ago the women weren't involved. When they did the sun dance, there was only one woman involved. She had to be an elderly woman that had lived a good life. She carried the pipe from the sweat lodge to the entrance of the dance circle, and then it was handed over to the men. A woman never pierced, never took flesh from herself. It was because she gave this world—she gives this world —flesh already, when she gives birth.

She suffers for the people, to make the nation.

These are the natural ways. And people nowadays are not doing it the right way. So they have all this turmoil going on—lightning hitting trees, trees breaking, and stuff like that—because of this. In the old times, women had their own ways and men had their ways. If it was meant for a woman to carry a pipe, then it would have been brought to the woman, but it wasn't. The calf pipe woman— the White Buffalo Woman—came and brought the pipe to the men.[3] It was a gift to the men to carry the pipe, and to protect and serve the family. The women had their own way. They were given a cleansing. They were given the power to make a nation grow in natural ways. That's why these things were kept separate, but now they're combining these different things, and there's confusion. That's why the old ways have to come back—the courting and the marriages and all that. It's gone, but the knowledge is there, and they don't understand that they have to keep it.

There are some *akíchitas* that are going to bring it back, bring it back the old way. I asked my mom to help explain to these women why we don't want them in the sun dance circle. It's not that we're being prejudiced. It's because we understand something that's deeper than white society has created.

The ones who run our sun dance always say that if someone brings them a pipe, you can't say no. The woman who brings a pipe and wants to sun dance—they can't say no. But if you bring a pipe to one *akíchita* who is running a sun dance, he will tell her no.

A young girl is used in the sun dance ceremony when they go to get the tree. They get the tree and bring it and then they stop four times on the way coming to the circle. After that, the young girl is not in that circle; the young girl is taken back.

OLIVIA: Way back, they had a lot of respect for one another. And they had so much respect that the Indian ladies wouldn't talk to their fathers-in-law, and fathers-in-law wouldn't talk to their daughters-in-law and the same with the son-in-law and the mother-in-law. If the father-in-law wanted to talk to the daughter-in-law, he would talk through the mother or another person and tell them to tell her, even if she was standing right there, listening.

The women always took care of the children and put up the tipis. They kind of spaced their children out and did not have as many as they do now, probably because they moved so much. I remember asking my grandpa something one time. I was changing the diaper of one of Esther's kids at the house, so I asked Grandpa in Lakota what they used instead of cloth years ago. He told me that they used the hide of an unborn calf. The women tanned it and made it soft. He said they made a diaper that you tied on the side with strings—something like a string. They'd take buffalo chips and pound that until it was almost powder-like, then they lined it on that hide and put the hide on the baby. And then, after they traveled a while, they took it and shook it out, and there was nothing on the hide.

ESTHER: So the women cared for the children all the time, and they taught them what they were doing. If they were pounding cherries and making patties, they'd have their little ones come out and help them to make patties. They'd see what the mothers were doing, and that's how they learned. And then if the woman was sewing or something, they would show it. The grandmothers were the ones that really worked with the children.

Like I said, it's very different now. Women are doing things outside the home.

AARON: There are a lot of things that women can be involved in—health, kids, putting something through law and stuff—I can see all that; it's coming. But in our traditional ways, I believe it should stay the same as it was a long time ago. When they started changing back in the late 1970s, everything became turmoil. Nowadays that turmoil is huge. You go to a sun dance and over half the dancers are women. And even in the sun dance, men and women don't respect each other. After the sun dance, they just lie all over the place. A long time ago women never did that. They were modest, and they stayed out of the center, and they never were out in public like the men. They were strong, because they gave birth to the nation, so their strength was supporting it.

Men had much more respect for women back in those days than they do now. The men long ago didn't talk about the women the way they do nowadays. For example, there's a woman that everybody was calling Crazy Woman, because she was involved in a lot of things like that. Not to disrespect her, but you know when people start saying things like that, it's kind of hard. My mom and my aunt have gained respect from people all over, just because they knew how to live their lives when they were young and growing up. Nowadays it's completely different, and what makes it worse, it tempts the young men.

HILDA: Do you want to tell something about modesty in the old days?

OLIVIA: Well, in the old days, they used to say we couldn't walk over anything—somebody's clothing, you can't walk over it—and you couldn't go in front of a man when you were having your period. When you have your period, you're also not supposed to be in the kitchen handling food.

You didn't dress in front of anybody. They wore long skirts. They didn't wear short skirts and show their legs. They were modest in that way. Now everybody wears shorts, but years ago, they didn't do it that way. They had self-respect. The women weren't even supposed to be heard. They always said that the man knew and did the talking.

HILDA: I noticed in that video of your parents, Ben and Ellen, when they were at my father's home, that Ellen sat with her head bowed down. My father spoke to her, but she didn't say anything.

OLIVIA: Mom was a quiet person. She was shy. She talked to us girls, you know, but she hardly talked to other people.

LORI: Back to the women's conduct—when they were walking, did they have to walk behind the man?

OLIVIA: Yeah, the Indian men would walk first, and then the women in back.

Years ago, they say that the Indian women did all the work. They chopped wood and they hauled water. When it was time to move camp, they were the ones that did the bundling up and getting the stuff together, took care of the kids and—

HILDA: It was pretty much that way with white women, too. Even now, when people move, the women do most of the packing. But today, men are helping more and more.

OLIVIA: They do the outside work. That's the way it was with me and my old man [husband]. We worked side by side in the fields, but he never did do anything in the house. I did all the housework.

ESTHER: Well, that's the tradition. The women did quite a bit, because the men went out to hunt. The men always walked first, and—

OLIVIA:—and the women carried the pack! You know, it was always the women who did the hardest work, because they did all the preserving of food, cooking, and raising the kids, but the man was out to get whatever. And a lot of the time the women didn't know whether or not the man was ever going to come back, because of being in a war. So they had to do all of those things themselves, learning butchering and hauling wood and starting fires.

LORI: Did they also help make decisions?

OLIVIA: Yeah, they did.

LORI: Did they ever have positions in the council?

ESTHER: They had councils. It was only the men [who could be in the council].

OLIVIA: But now women are getting involved in things—the council and everything. I think a woman is more apt to have the leadership of doing things now, talking out more than a man would.

LORI: You talked, when we first met, about how uncles and aunts would take responsibility for teaching certain things. Could you tell about that now?

AARON: In the family, the uncles and aunts were the ones that raised the children, teaching them the things that they needed to know. Grandpa Ben and Uncle Hank and our uncles on my grandpa's side taught us how to dance and do the ceremonies. My Uncle Hank took us out and taught us how to hunt. The grandparents taught the young kids. When you're young and growing up, you have a tendency to watch your grandparents instead of your mom and dad. That's why I always went to my Grandpa Bill and Grandpa Ben, and I had a tendency to be drawn to my Uncle Jim.

ESTHER: The wisdom and the knowledge of their past was handed down to the children. And it was always verbal, never in writing. If they knew something about the past that was real important, or that they thought was important to them, they'd tell their grandchildren, or even their children. It's handed down.

AARON: It's just like Grandpa Bill Horn Cloud or Grandpa Moses. The things they told me were all handed down. Nowadays we live in different worlds, really three worlds—we have to live in the old way; we have to live the reservation way; then, too, we have to live the European way. In their time, they had two ways.

LORI: Is that the way you see the future playing out? Can you learn how to bring the traditions in?

AARON: Well, the way I see the future, it is not that way. The way I see it is the Indians now are having so much trouble with their ceremonies. They don't realize that mixing a lot of things from Europe, and modern things, into their old-time ceremonies is causing their disruption.

As I have said, women have something that's very natural that men don't have. Women have the gift to make the nation grow, to give birth. But they also have a cleansing that people don't like to talk about—it's hard to talk about it—and that's a woman's own personal time. Men don't have that; that's why they have the sweat lodge. When you have that idea and understanding, you should never mix them, because when you mix them, it just hurts a lot of people. And now it's hurting people all over this world.

When a woman is at that time of the month, they always stay away from men. It can create sickness. That's what makes men get weaker and weaker. In order to build a nation, you have to have both men and women. When one creates sickness in the other, then that nation dies.

ESTHER: Like when they have the sun dance. At that time of the month, women don't go in there.

OLIVIA: Mind you, if a person does have her period and goes in there, those dancers and the spiritual leader know it. And it's embarrassing. The person who has her period had better leave, because they'll come and just pick her right up and take her, because they got her pointed out.

AARON: A long time ago, when you were in that cycle you wouldn't come near the sun dance. You had to stay away at other camps. So even today when they have a sun dance and somebody has her time, they tell her, "Go get a motel or something. Go watch television. Don't come to the sun dance. Stay away."

OLIVIA: Years ago, they used to say *išnáthi,* meaning the woman had to be alone for four days. So years ago, when they said *išnáthi,* you knew that that person had her period, and they made her stay away in a little lodge, or wherever, until it was over.

HILDA: Wasn't that a kind of punishment?

OLIVIA: No, no!

AARON: When you have that time of the month, things come to you—that's why you spend that time alone. A man has that time, too. He goes up and spends four days on a hill. Nobody comes around him while he stays up there and prays.

ESTHER: And then when a woman has that time—her period—they never step on her clothes.

OLIVIA: On her clothes or anything—or go near her.

AARON: And during that time, they weren't supposed to wash dishes or cook.

OLIVIA: Those things weren't taught; those were natural things that came within the people.

LORI: When did these traditions end, and when have they started again, or have they continued?

OLIVIA: With the really traditional people, it's still there. It's still there.

And when a woman has her change of life—that's another thing again.

AARON: It's when the gift that Tunkashila gave you to create life for the nation is taken from you.

OLIVIA: You have to be strong, because you get signs: you get hot flashes and a side effect and all that. But then the Indian way is, you have to be strong. You have to have a strong mind and a strong heart, and you've got to go on with what you're doing and not give up, because when you give up, you're weakening yourself. Nowadays when a woman goes through the change of life, she has to see a psychiatrist, or she has to have all kinds of estrogens and everything.

AARON: It's just like there are seven ways with the pipe, and there's one for women. The first time she has her cycle, they put her in a tipi, and she prays with the pipe and she has things for a woman to do. And the older women go in and instruct her on how to make clothes, and how to cook, and they talk about her cycle and what she has to do—how to keep away from people during the time she cleanses herself.

The men are taught by men. The women are taught by women. Nowadays, because of the white society, the women have to teach the children. But that's where the *thiyóšpaye* comes in.

LORI: So even though you express the fact that your mom really didn't talk much, I mean, in spiritual matters; she still had a lot of things, traditions, that she told you about?

ESTHER: I have talked to my two girls, and they know about it. I don't know whether they will carry it on, when my other daughter has children. But they learn from their aunts, too.

AARON: Just like us boys; we have to teach our nephews.

Part 3. Grandfather Black Elk

We Remember

Throughout our conversations, whenever the subject of Black Elk as grandfather was brought up, Esther and Olivia brightened and looked almost like young girls again, for their memories of Black Elk are happy ones. Esther is four years older than Olivia, and can therefore remember more about their grandfather and early events.

LORI: What do you remember about your grandfather, [Nicholas] Black Elk?

OLIVIA: Oh, I can remember when we were little and lived with Mom and Dad near Manderson. We were so happy when we looked from our house down the road toward Manderson and saw Grandpa and Grandma coming in their wagon!

ESTHER: We were always playing outside, and we always noticed when a wagon went by. We knew who they were. And pretty soon, here they would come. They had one horse that was a pinto and the other one was a black horse; that was their team. And when you saw those two coming, you knew it was Grandma and Grandpa. So as soon as we saw them coming, well, we just beat it down to the road!

We'd get down to the gate about the time they'd reach it. We were tickled to see them. We all jumped into the back end of the wagon and came up to the house.

Most of the time it was in the summertime, when they came. In the wintertime, we went to school at Holy Rosary. Sometimes they came to see us at school, but not much, because it was so far.

Our grandparents were the ones that usually kept us in line, telling us what to do and telling us stories and talking to us about what we

should do and what we shouldn't do. If we were naughty or something, they'd tell us that we shouldn't do that. And they'd talk in a
nice way. They never hollered at us. They were generous. It seemed
like they were always happy, because every time they'd come we
would all talk and laugh. Sometimes we didn't see them for maybe
two weeks or something like that, but that's a long way to come in
a wagon.

HILDA: You were talking about when the interviews for *Black Elk
Speaks* were going on in the tipi at your grandparents' home. Do you
want to tell about that now?

OLIVIA: They were all in a tent and talking. I was only about four or
five. I remember this: I threw that flap open, I just threw it open, like
this, and I ran in. And my dad just grabbed me and he just put me
right back out again!

HILDA: That was in May 1931. Esther was eight and remembers listening, too.

ESTHER: Oh, yeah! I'd sit there and listen to them talk, because the
words sounded like rhymes, music—a rhythm. Pretty soon my dad
was going like this, waving with his hand for me to go, or they'd say,
"Go play; go on and help your mother or something." I'd get up and
go, and I'd come back around and sit down again when they didn't
notice. I had to take them coffee, you know. Mom was giving me the
cups and I'd take the coffee and pour it out very slow, just to listen
to them.

What fascinated me was the rhythm in the way my grandfather
talked in Lakota. It just had a rhythm, the way he talked. And then
the way my dad brought it out in English, it rhymed now and then.
The language sounded like a rhythm. I always wanted to bring the
coffee to them, because I wanted to listen. That's what fascinated
me—just the way he talked. In Steltenkamp's book, he mentioned
something about Neihardt being a poet, that he put the words the
way he wanted them.[1] Well, poetry's what I got out of it, the way it
sounded when he spoke.

LORI: As you look at *Black Elk Speaks,* does it ring true to your memory
of what you heard during the interviews?

ESTHER: Oh, yes! I read it, part of it. Remember, Hilda, we were up on the hill that time and were talking about the book? I thought, "Well, I better read it." I didn't finish it then. There were so many things I had to do. Every now and then I'd read, then some other books came up, and I'd sit and read those. Everybody was saying, "Remember that book by Steltenkamp?" I thought I'd better read that book all the way through, because I knew about the others.

LORI: Do you remember hearing your grandfather or your father talk about John Neihardt? I mean, after he did the book. Did they mention what they'd done in the book?

ESTHER: Well, every now and then, but not very often. I was going to school then, so it was just in the summertime when I was home.

OLIVIA: Another thing I remember about Grandpa: I remember the pageant Grandpa was in.[2] About 1937, five or six families went to the Black Hills and were in it with him. I remember the Iron Hawks were there, and Aunt Lucy and the family of her husband, Leo Looks Twice. George Looks Twice was there. We went up there three summers straight. The first summer, I can hardly remember. I know I must have been about ten years old.

The pageant started out with dancing and a powwow. They did the grass dance and the kettle dance.

HILDA: Who did the grass dance?

OLIVIA: The men did. Uncle Leo was a singer and he was a drummer, he and his brothers, Roy and Reuben. They really had pretty voices. Everybody on the reservation used to think they were real good singers.

Anyway, at the pageant, we used to start in the morning. We were in a round building, and it looked like there was sand on the floor, and they had a sun dance tree inside that round building. I can't really remember what happened first, but I remember them doing the sun dance, the way they sang and the way they danced. But it wasn't the real thing—it was a pageant.

And then they did the ritual of a dead person—how they put them on a scaffold. And that was me—I was always the dead person. I was little, so they put me up on the scaffold. They wrapped me up in a buffalo robe. I remember one time someone had given me a big round piece of bubble gum, and just as they were lifting me to the scaffold, I blew a big bubble! My dad really got after me about that!

We lived way down in a canyon in a camp, and they hauled water to us. Farther down there was Crystal Cave. The camp was really nice. We took showers up on the hill and we had a place to wash our clothes.

Our father was part of the pageant—he danced. I don't think he did the sun dance, but he danced traditional. I remember how we all had to take care of our costumes. My brother Benjamin Jr. was about four when he took part in the pageant. He was a good dancer, and he really had a nice outfit. My other brother, Henry, helped him to make it. The back of his outfit had two bustles, one high and one low. My mom made him the cuffs, and I think Mama made him the apron. His apron was made of velvet, black. He had a whole black outfit, with white beads. It was a really outstanding outfit that he had. I think they gave it away when he died.

HILDA: What did you think of Mr. Duhamel?

OLIVIA: He was a really nice man. He was a pleasant man. He was good to the Indians; he got them whatever they needed, and he kept the water supply going, which was good. My dad and the Duhamels were really good friends. Even after the pageant, my dad used to go and see Bud Duhamel [Alex Duhamel's son], and Bud's always asking for us and wondering what we're doing.

ESTHER: We all liked Alex Duhamel.

HILDA: When you went to Duhamel's pageant, how did you travel?

OLIVIA: I remember them coming after us in a truck, because people had everything with them, their bedding and all that. If I remember right, about three or four families went and we rode with them. My dad had a little Model A Ford car, and we couldn't get all that stuff in there. I remember my brother rode with them, and Grace, my sister, and Esther and I, and it might have been Kate. Anyway, we rode in a truck, and we really enjoyed it, because it was open, and we could just see everything

HILDA: When you went up to the Black Hills, did you feel that you were going to a sacred place that you had heard about?

OLIVIA: Yes. Grandpa used to show us where they got their wood and their lodge poles, and then they used to do the sun dance in certain places in the Black Hills. That was when Grandpa was younger. The sun dance he told about was way back in the Hills—over here by Smithwick, in that direction.

ESTHER: Different people went up there to the pageant, not just us. We'd go up the hill from the camp in a panel truck in the morning, when it was still chilly. The road was curvy all the way, and the people would sing all the way up. We sang: "It's hard to be an Indian. Anyway, have courage!" Even some of us cried. It was hard in those days.

In the pageant, they did different dances, like the kettle dance, in all the shows. In the old times when they did the kettle dance, they had meat cooking in a kettle over a fire, and they danced around it. But in the pageant they did not really have anything cooking in the pot; they just danced around it.

OLIVIA: I remember that the pageant started with hoop dancing and then the eagle dance and the buffalo dance, and then they performed a kind of sun dance. I was little, so they put me up on the scaffold. What was that scaffold about anyway?

ESTHER: It showed how they buried dead people, but they didn't perform the whole ceremony. In the olden days, they put a person on the scaffold because they didn't know if he was really dead; he might have been in a coma.

The show would tell how the Indians did things in the old days.

OLIVIA: It was a pageant for tourists. We performed, and we did the acting.

HILDA: What did your grandfather do?

ESTHER: Well, he just got up and showed how they did things in the old days. For example, he put Olivia up on that scaffold, and then he'd tell about their lives and what they believed.

LORI: Were what was shown in the pageant actually sacred ceremonies?

ESTHER: No, they wouldn't do that.

LORI: You mentioned something about a New Year's dance and your grandfather.

ESTHER: Well, my grandma and grandpa used to come in a wagon, and they were getting ready to have a New Year's dance in Manderson. So the people were all coming in and the snow was deep. And so we got in the wagon and helped them. As you go in a wagon, the wheels squeak; they make that funny noise on the snow. You could just hear that, and it would be getting kind of dusklike when they came. Well, we went over there to help, and we had to clear the snow away out where they were in camp. They wanted to camp close to the building there, so we had it all cleared out and we had a fire going. Then we pitched a tent up and they put hay all around the sides for people to sleep on inside the tent. And the stove was right in the middle. That's how we did it in the wintertime; nowadays you just go in a car and enjoy yourself. Those were wagon days.

We usually went for maybe two or three days. It was a log building where they had the dance. They even had bleachers—they were logs—and that's where they sat. They had a stove that was a barrel fixed up for a stove. They used to dance all dressed up in their costumes, and they had clowns that came in. And they danced the old year out and danced the New Year in. Some of the clowns would be dressed drab—like old people—and then some of them would come in with a diaper and a bottle. They had a lot of fun. They did that ever since I can remember, before I was even eleven or twelve years old. Then they quit. They didn't have a building.

ESTHER: When I stayed with my grandpa at White Horse Creek, they had a regular house. It was a log house, like one we have up on the hill, just one big room. And I can always remember they had a round table with claws on it. I used to sit and look at them. Those were bear claws or something. My Aunt Lucy used to make cake. That's the first thing I always wanted, was to clean out the bowl with the cake mix. Aunt Lucy baked from scratch.

Aunt Lucy and Leo lived way out in the back. We used to go out there, in those days, and they had a chicken coop and chickens. I can always remember a pine tree there where my grandfather used to sit and talk to us and tell us things and teach us.

I don't know if it's still there.

ESTHER: I remember something that happened when I was about ten or twelve years old. It must have been in the springtime; it wasn't cold, anyway. I happened to be home, because my mother was sick, and I stayed home all week to help out. I was at my grandfather's house, and he was sitting down, getting his pipe ready early in the morning, and here was Father Sialm knocking on the door.[3] They opened the door, and he came in, and he saw my grandfather with the pipe. Father Sialm grabbed the pipe and said, "This is the work of the devil!" And he took it and threw it out the door on the ground.

My grandfather didn't say a word. He got up and took the priest's prayer book and threw it out on the ground. Then they both looked at each other, and nobody said one word that whole time.

And then they both went out, and I saw Father Sialm pick up the prayer book, and Grandfather picked up his pipe. Each one picked up his own.

Then they turned around, and they just smiled at each other and shook hands!

Then they went back in the house.

OLIVIA: I heard, too, that once my grandpa was in a tipi, trying to heal a little boy, when a priest came in. Grandpa was using a rattle in the ceremony, and the priest took it, threw it out of the tipi, and stamped on it. He told Grandpa not to do heathen things like that, and he whipped Grandpa out of the tipi. That's in a book, too. A man told me.

ESTHER: One time when my brother Banjo [Benjamin Jr.] was little—he must have been about four years old—we used to have these big dishpans; they had handles on the side. My brother was sleigh riding on that dishpan, back and forth. He was out there talking loud to my grandfather about something.

From the house I could see that Grandpa was arguing with my brother. He kept shaking his head. Finally we looked, and here he got in that dishpan! Grandpa got in there, and he could hardly cross his legs. My brother told him to go, and he was trying to push. He couldn't do it, so my brother got down, put his foot on Grandpa's back and gave him a shove.

So we ran out to see what was going on, and Grandpa was spinning down the hill—spinning around and around in that dishpan! Pretty soon he fell off, and went in the snow. We were all laughing, and Grandpa came up, and he said in Lakota language, "I'm not going to do that anymore." He was mad about it, at my little brother.

CLIFTON: I was born the second of January in the blizzard of 1949.
ESTHER: We came down here to Pine Ridge on New Year's Eve to the hospital. Clifton was supposed to be born on Christmas, but I was overdue. There was a blizzard, and you couldn't see anything. The whole side of the hospital was covered, even the windows, clear down from the top. They had to move all the patients to one side of the hospital. Then the nurses couldn't come across from their houses. The ones that were on duty that night had to stay through the storm. They had different patients who could get around to do the cleaning. They needed some things sterilized, so I told them, "I can do that." So I went and sterilized whatever they needed, and then I had others making cotton balls.

Finally the weather let up, and we were still there. Father Zimmerman came and said, "I just came from Manderson."[4] I asked, "How are the roads?" "Oh, I just went up and down the hillside, and the roads were all high-packed with snow banks," he replied. Just then my husband came in, and I asked Father Zimmerman if we [my husband, the baby, and I] could come home with him. I asked the doctor if I could be discharged, and he said, "All right." So we headed home.

We got in Father Zimmerman's car, and honestly, this snow bank, it was so high that he drove along the edges. We went way up on the hillside where it was bare and bounced all over the place. We came down where it was bare on the road, and then again—where there were snow banks—we had to go clear up on the hillside again. We kept doing that until we got home.

When we got in the house, Grandpa was sitting there, and he had a quilt over him. My husband always hollered when he went in, "Hi, Grandpa!" And he rubbed Grandpa's hands, and his hands were ice-cold. Grandpa said in Lakota, "Now I'm going to be warm." They had just woken up, and that house was so cold.

And then I told him about the baby. I'd come back with him. So Grandpa held out his arms, and he held him. He was holding Clifton, and he was singing to him while we were trying to put wood in the stove and get it warm in there.

Byron was just little then. He heard us, and he came running out of that room. And Olivia was there, watching Byron. So Grandpa held my two oldest ones on his lap.

So Clifton can say, "I was in my great-grandpa's arms!"

ESTHER: My husband and I would come to Grandpa's and sit and talk. My husband can speak Lakota, but he doesn't like to carry on a conversation with anybody. We'd come and we'd sit by my grandfather, and we'd ask him a few questions, because we wanted to know different things. And one time Grandpa told us—and this is even before they had those clustered houses coming in to Pine Ridge and on the reservation—he said, "There's going to be houses coming—square houses." And he said, "There's going to be drinking and fighting, and then something's going to come in. I don't know, but it's going to make their minds whirl, and they'll be worse. They'll even use clubs or things like that, killing each other."

We never thought anything about it. We thought he was just saying that. Then one day my husband and I were sitting at home, and he said, "Remember that time Grandpa told us about these square houses and the drinking and the fighting and quarreling? And he said something was going to come that would work on their minds until they were twirling around? Well, I think we have it here now. We've got square houses, and we've got alcohol, and they're always fighting. And now we've got drugs, and that's what he was talking about—it ruined their minds."

You know, I never thought of it until we were sitting there talking at the table. That's what Grandpa told us that one time, and that's what he meant.

Grandfather's Healing

LORI: Do you remember anything about your grandfather's work as a holy man? Anything about his healing of sick persons?

OLIVIA: When he did healing, he never did it with closed doors or in darkness. He healed wherever they needed him. He did a lot of healing ceremonies at night, with his hands and with herbs.

Grandpa did some healing one time—I must have been about eleven or twelve. I didn't witness the ceremony, but I heard them talking. This man, Pretty Hip, from Porcupine, couldn't urinate, and there was something wrong with him. They took him all over and they finally brought him to Grandpa for medicine. They had to watch this man all night long, because of the medicine that Grandpa gave him. And he was suffering, really suffering. I think this man probably had kidney stones, because when Grandpa gave him this medicine—about four o'clock in the morning, just as it was daybreak—this guy had to go to the bathroom. So he went, and if he didn't pass those stones—but that's what he did. That is one time I know of Grandpa doing that. About two or three days after that happened, they took my grandpa down there to Porcupine and they had a *wóphila,* a thanksgiving dinner, for my grandpa, and they gave him all kinds of gifts. Esther, did you ever hear that?

ESTHER: Yes. Another time—I must have been seven or eight years old—when it was night, they brought a little girl in to his home. I don't remember what was wrong with her at the time, but they had her in there, and Grandpa prayed. With the *yuwípis,* it's supposed to be dark. This time Grandpa had lamps lit; it was light. And he had this rattle; it was a turtle. He was going around and it sounded like a weasel or raccoons coming out of his back.

OLIVIA: It wasn't a growling sound; it was more like a blow. You know, when a horse blows?

ESTHER: And I was really surprised. I kept trying to listen. And that noise—a kind of chirping, chattering, like a little animal. It sounded like it came right from his back. He danced all around with that rattle and was singing, and then he prayed, and then he had some kind of medicine.

LORI: Did the little girl get well?

ESTHER: Yes. One day, after I got older, I asked him about this little girl. I never did ask what was wrong with her, but that noise stuck in my mind, so I asked him. He said, "When they do a ceremony, the animals help." They helped him.

And so I asked, "How come you had all the lights on?" I had heard about this other ceremony, called *yuwípi*, where it's supposed to be dark—you see sparks and all that. I asked him about the lights, and he said, "No, that's different from a medicine man. *Yuwípi* is different. A medicine man doesn't have to sit in the dark and do things. The medicine man does it in the light. If it's at night, they light a lamp. And they even do it in the daytime."

OLIVIA: He used to blow like that. He would blow on whatever he was doing. That I remember. Blow—a really blow hard—that horse-blowing sound. We don't know if it came from him or if the spirits did it.

Afterward he passed the pipe around, and I always wanted to sneak in there so I could smoke!

Then they would have a kind of feast. The people who brought the sick person also brought the food. And now, they still do that.

Grandpa didn't live with us when he was doing all this, so we really don't know a lot, but sometimes we would witness one [a healing], or hear talk about it. He was a healer. He healed with herbs.

ESTHER: I went to a healer, Pete Catches. All the time he was fixing his things, he was talking. He said the same thing as my grandfather did. "When I heal or repair anything like that," he said, "I do not do it in the dark. If it's at night, I always have the lights on, and if I do it in the daytime, it's all daylight."

OLIVIA: And then Grandpa used to say, too, "Tunkashila—it's not me, but Tunkashila that's doing that. He's the one that's doing the healing. I'm not doing it. He's doing it through me." That's the way I understood this healing.

OLIVIA: I witnessed another healing of my grandfather's at one time at our house. I was just a little girl then, too, probably nine or ten. They took this girl to the hospital, and she was pregnant, but she had a tubal pregnancy, and they told her she was losing the baby. And so they came to Grandpa. I don't really remember how he performed that, but he put the baby in the uterus. And they were really amazed at it because Miss Wallace, the nurse, took this girl to the hospital, and she had a normal baby. And the doctor was really questioning. I remember they came and got Aunt Lucy and Miss Wallace and questioned Grandpa about it. "How did he do that?" And he didn't tell. Grandpa didn't understand any English at all, so we had to tell him in Lakota.

HILDA: Some say that Black Elk spoke some English.

OLIVIA: No, he didn't talk any English.

I remember another time Grandpa did some healing. It was when we were at the Duhamel pageant camp in the Black Hills. We all went up there. Henry Horse was the patient's name.[1] There was something wrong with his stomach. They took him to the hospital, and they said he was dying, so they brought him to Duhamel's pageant camp. Grandpa did not know that Henry Horse was in bad shape. They told Grandpa that Henry Horse was dying. Grandpa said, "No, no!" He went down to Spring Creek and got some herbs and came back, and I think he boiled the herbs and gave them to Henry Horse to drink. I remember my mother said he was very gentle and scooped the herbs up with a spoon and fed them to him.

Then Grandpa had a ceremony, did rattling, did blowing, and he prayed to the four directions. Grandpa stayed all day with Henry Horse in a tent. The next morning, Henry Horse sat up, and he was all right.

From healing, our conversations went to Black Elk's religious beliefs as he had told or revealed them to his granddaughters.

OLIVIA: Every evening, we used to sit down, and he would pray and smoke the pipe, passing the pipe around the family. I was only nine years old then, but I used to look forward to smoking a pipe. After he got converted to the church, we took the rosary in Lakota almost every night.

ESTHER: Every morning and every night he prayed. And then when he walked he used to take the rosary and pray the rosary. He knew how to say the rosary—the Hail Mary—in Indian, and then the Our Father in Indian. He was reading from that prayer book that was all written in Indian. Father Buechel had translated the prayers into Indian. My grandfather picked up the book, and he read that Indian just like he had schooling already. And that's why I always ask, "How in the world did he learn how to read Indian?" When he'd go to church, he'd be sitting there, and he'd have his Indian prayer book, and he'd read it. He'd read it and the rest of them would answer. And he would just pray Indian in church.

HILDA: When you told about being asked to speak in the school about the Indian religion, you mentioned something about your grandfather's saying there is a similarity between the Christian religion and the Indian's.

ESTHER: There is a similarity. That's what my grandfather said. We believe in the same person up above. You can pray any place, regardless of where you are. You don't have to go to the church and pray, like on Sundays. That is not necessary.

He said, "You can go even up the hill someplace and pray. You can sit and talk to the wind, the trees, and they kind of make that sound, like they're talking back to you." "And," he said, "you can look down at the ground and those rocks. They roll, too. They're living, too." That's what he said. "And so why go to church, then?" I asked him. "No," he said, "you can go to church and pray. You can go pray."

It's amazing how he really caught on to things. He used to have his rosary, and he would go down the road to Manderson, to the post office or to the store there, and keep saying his rosary in Lakota. Then he would come back. But when he was home, in the morning, he got up and prayed with his pipe, and in the evening he prayed with his pipe.

He used to sit and talk with us. He used to say, "You have to be good listeners. Any place you go, if you listen, you will learn. It sticks in your mind. Your mind is like a book."

So I asked him one time in the Lakota language, "How come you go to church, then you come back and pray with the pipe?" He said, "We all pray to the same Wakhą́ Thą́ka, Great Spirit. We can pray anywhere, any place, any way, whatever we use, even if it's symbols. The church has symbols. They have statues, their own symbols. Our pipe is a symbol, and we respect it."

You know, it makes sense.

Caring for Grandfather

OLIVIA: I didn't get to be with my grandfather enough when I was young. When I was home from school, he was always at his house, and it was a long trip by wagon to where he lived. Of course, we were always glad to see him when he and Grandma came over. I remember how we girls would sing songs with our grandfather. Grandpa sang a lot of songs. He was a person that we really loved. We really and truly loved him, and he in turn loved us. When we were in school at Holy Rosary, he would come there, and I remember I went over to hold his hand. When we kids saw him coming, we would run and meet him. There were quite a few of us that were his grandchildren!

I remember that Grandpa walked to Manderson often. We taught him to say Manderson, so we would know where he was going, but the way he said it, it sounded more like "medicine."

But toward the end, when he was getting too old, Grandpa was with us. Aunt Lucy had him first. When she took care of him, she was at his place, but before long she couldn't do it anymore, and she asked my dad to take over. My dad went and brought him back to our house. Mom was the one who wanted to keep him. She said it was a woman's job to tend to an elder.

When he came to our place, Grandpa didn't want to be among the kids, because, he said, "I'm getting old now." He told my dad that he wanted to live by himself. First, he wanted to live in a tent like in the old days, but my dad said it was too cold. So my dad got the agency to build a little one-room house for him, right where the homestead is and where Esther lives now, and that's where he stayed. There was heat in the house, and it looked nice and comfortable all the way through. I lived with my folks in the log house.

At that point, Grandpa could hardly walk. We did take him to a hospital, and the doctor said he was getting old and we would have to put him in a home. But Papa did not want to do that. He said we would take care of him. Grandpa was bedridden. Henry was home from the service, and he helped us. Esther and her family were in Belle Fourche, South Dakota, so my sister, Grace, and Henry and my mother and I took care of him. We put him in pajamas, changed the bed every day, and kept him clean. I was about twenty-three years old then.

Grandpa did a lot of praying—with the rosary in Lakota and with the pipe.

He got so bad; he got so weak. We took turns staying with him at night and in the daytime. He would talk sometimes, and other times he wouldn't say anything.

Grandpa didn't hurt. I would ask him, "Grandpa, do you hurt any place?" He'd shake his head, no. Then he got to the point where he couldn't talk. He was always wanting a rosary in his hands. I could see that sometimes he must have been praying, because he would move. He had his pipe, but toward the end Aunt Lucy had his pipe. I don't know if she took his pipe or if Dad gave it to her, but she had his pipe.

HILDA: I remember that when Black Elk told about hunting buffalo, he'd say, "I wish I had some of that meat now!" Did he ever get buffalo meat when you were taking care of him?
OLIVIA: Oh, yes. We used to go up in the Black Hills, to Custer, in the state park, and when they killed buffalo up there, my dad would bring some home. We cooked it for Grandpa. Then when he got so he couldn't eat the meat, we had to grind it for him. Toward the end, we bought baby food—that toddler food. That's what we fed him. He was paralyzed, and we had to water the food down so that it was kind of soupy, so he'd be able to swallow.
HILDA: Lucy told me that before your grandfather died, several family members were with him, and he told them that your traditional religion—the pipe religion—was what he really believed and wanted them to follow. Do you think that is correct?
OLIVIA: Well, to me, yes—I think that's correct, because he always

prayed with the pipe. Whether he was a converted Catholic or what, he always had the pipe, and he was praying with it. Of course, he prayed in Lakota all the time.

My father told us that sometime before Grandpa died, he said this: "When I die, something will happen."

OLIVIA: Two or three days before he died, we knew he was going, because he could not keep water or soup down. We knew it was coming, and my brother Henry stayed all the time in the little house with him. He stayed there at night, and one night he came to our log home and said, "I think you girls had better get over there." So my dad and all of us went over there.

When we went in the little house, my brother Henry was holding Grandpa like a baby. Then Grandpa just went away. He died in Henry's arms.

After he died, they took him and they embalmed him, and it was the next night that we had the wake. We kept him in the house, and all the relations gathered. Everybody came and sat around in the little house. A lot of them sat outside, and it was just moonlight outside. It was really a nice night, and it was just the night to sit, warm and with a wind.

All of a sudden it started to get light, and it was almost like daylight, and the northern lights were dancing! That scared me. I thought it was the end of the world, the way the whole thing was just lit up! It scared us half to death! Those lights were dancing like fire!

OLIVIA: We did not take Grandfather to the church. We had services right there at the house, at our home. He had a nice funeral. It was both Catholic and traditional, because we had Frank Good Lance, a holy man from Kyle, there to pray with the pipe. We buried him in the cemetery on the hill in Manderson.

Afterword

One summer day, during the last of our conversations for this book, we were at Olivia's home on the Pine Ridge Reservation at the edge of the Badlands near Porcupine, South Dakota.

Our talking had slowed for the moment, and all was quiet except for the whir of a window fan.

Olivia sat in a chair near the center of the room. Her feet were resting on a stool, for she was recovering from a recent knee operation.

Esther stood at the far end of the living room, half leaning against the wall. A hand held against her right cheek emphasized her deeply thoughtful mood. Then she spoke, and her quiet words revealed the thought that possessed her.

"You know, they say he was converted, but—"

As though the idea had originally been hers, Olivia broke in, "—but he already knew the holiness of everything—the earth, the sun, the moon and the stars—everything! Grandpa was already a holy man!"

Appendix

The Black Elk Family Tree

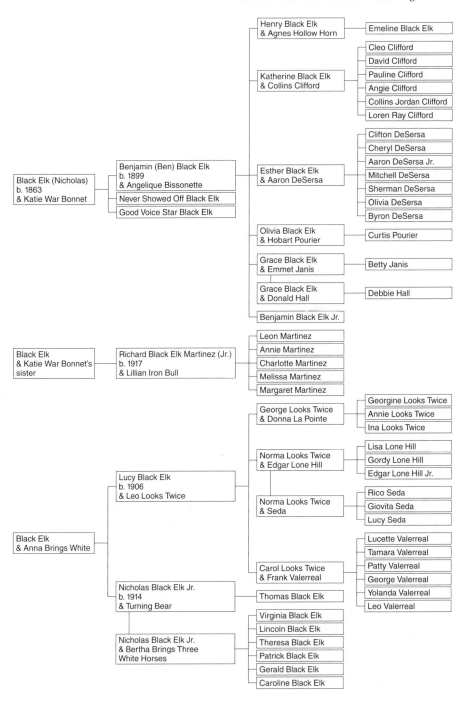

Notes

Editors' Preface

1. Dr. Littleton, then academic dean at Stephens College in Columbia, Missouri, had in 1977 invited Black Elk's daughter, Lucy Looks Twice, to speak to the students at the college. She did so on 7 April 1977.

2. Essay by Neihardt in his column "Of Making Books," *St. Louis Dispatch,* 20 June 1931.

Introduction

1. Because many diverse systems have been used to write Lakota, the Lakota words used throughout this book have in most cases been systematically transcribed to conform to the DeMallie-Parks system of orthography used by the American Indian Research Institute at Indiana University.

2. *Black Elk Speaks: Being the Life Story of a Holy Man of the Oglala Sioux,* as told through John Neihardt, Bison Books edition (Lincoln: University of Nebraska Press, 1988), p. 270.

3. The other Teton tribes are Hunkpapa, Sicanu (Brulé), Itazipco (Sans Arc), Minneconjou, Oohenumpa (Two Kettles), and Sihaspa (Blackfeet).

4. In terms of families with combined income below the federally defined poverty line.

5. Neihardt, *Black Elk Speaks,* p. 2.

The Legacy

1. Good Thunder was one of four men sent by the Lakotas to meet Wovoka, the Northern Paiute whose visions led to the ghost dance movement, and report back to the tribe.

2. Neihardt's reason for going to Pine Ridge Reservation was related to the book he had just begun, *The Song of the Messiah* (published as part of *A Cycle of the West* [Lincoln: University of Nebraska Press, 1991], pp. 419–505), an account of the ghost dance movement. He wished to become acquainted with

a Lakota holy man who had been a participant. In Black Elk he found what he was searching for—and more.

3. Joseph Epes Brown became interested in Black Elk through his reading of *Black Elk Speaks.* He later met Black Elk (ca. 1947), interviewed him, and wrote *The Sacred Pipe,* which was first published in 1953. A revised edition is available as *The Gift of the Sacred Pipe: Based on Black Elk's Account of the Seven Rites of the Oglala Sioux,* ed. and illus. Vera Louise Drysdale (Norman: University of Oklahoma Press, 1982).

4. The Wounded Knee Massacre took place on 29 December 1890, near the present town of Wounded Knee on Pine Ridge Reservation. For more information on the Wounded Knee Massacre, see William Coleman, *Voices of Wounded Knee* (Lincoln: University of Nebraska Press, 2000), and Richard Jensen, R. Eli Paul, and John E. Carter, eds., *Eyewitness at Wounded Knee* (Lincoln: University of Nebraska Press, 1991).

5. Wovoka, a Northern Paiute, had visions of a new world to come for Indian people, the interpretation of which grew into the ghost dance movement. For a detailed look at Wovoka's life, see Michael Hittman, *Wovoka and the Ghost Dance,* expanded edition (Lincoln: University of Nebraska Press, 1997). A classic overview of the ghost dance movement is James Mooney's *The Ghost-Dance Religion and the Sioux Outbreak of 1890* (Lincoln: University of Nebraska Press, 1991).

6. Neihardt, *Black Elk Speaks,* p. 270.

7. Selections are from Neihardt, *Black Elk Speaks,* pp. 253, 257, 259, 260, 261, and 270, and *The Song of the Messiah* in *A Cycle of the West,* p. 504.

8. *How the West Was Won,* Metro-Goldwyn-Mayer, 1962.

9. Neihardt, *Black Elk Speaks,* p. 6.

Father and Grandfather

1. *Heyokas* did everything backward, and they were considered holy men. They were like jokers or jesters, and their duty was to bring happiness to the people.

2. The Black Elk family performed during the Duhamel pageant in Keystone, South Dakota.

3. Ben Black Elk was speaking and being photographed at Keystone, South Dakota, where he appeared for twenty-seven years.

Growing Up

1. Olivia is referring to when the Neihardts visited during the 1931 interviews.

2. "Tree ears," a word for shelf fungus.

3. Esther and Olivia are recalling an advertisement for a detergent, Gold Dust, which was popular at that time.

A Life for the Community

1. The Public Health Service Hospital in Pine Ridge, South Dakota.

Reclaiming the Legacy

1. Baptiste Pourier (1843–1928), also known as Big Bat, was a famous scout and interpreter. He participated in many military events, including Crook's fight on the Rosebud on 17 June 1876.

2. Black Elk Heritage, Inc. is a South Dakota not-for-profit corporation whose purpose is to create a Black Elk Memorial Museum.

The Honor of a Pipe

1. Lucy Black Elk Looks Twice's daughter, Norma, gave the pipe to playwright Christopher Sergel at Lucy's funeral give-away. After his death, Gayle Sergel, his widow, returned it to the Black Elk family.

On the Front Lines

1. The Wounded Knee occupation in 1973 attracted widespread national attention. Members of the American Indian Movement (AIM) and others occupied the Wounded Knee trading post for seventy-one days, from February to May of 1973. Two Indians were killed, and both the store and a nearby Catholic Church were burned. See Rolland Dewing, *Wounded Knee: The Meaning and Significance of the Second Incident* (New York: Irvington, 1985). For an outsider's account of the occupation, see Stanley David Lyman, *Wounded Knee 1973: A Personal Account* (Lincoln: University of Nebraska Press, 1991). For a more complete look at Indian activism at that time and its long-term effects, see Alvin M. Josephy Jr., Joane Nagel, and Troy Johnson, eds., *Red Power: The American Indians' Fight for Freedom,* 2d ed. (Lincoln: University of Nebraska Press, 1999).

Working

1. Tensions about the selling of alcohol in White Clay, Nebraska, erupted in the summer of 1999. Two Lakota men were found murdered near White

Clay in June of that year, a crime that precipitated protest rallies and marches in White Clay. The first of these marches in late June turned violent, with protesters smashing windows, looting a local grocery store, and squaring off with the Nebraska State Patrol and tribal police.

2. For a look at the contemporary economy and society of the Lakotas, see Elizabeth S. Grobsmith, *Lakota of the Rosebud: A Contemporary Ethnography* (New York: Holt, Rinehart, and Winston, 1981), and Kathleen Ann Pickering, *Lakota Culture, World Economy* (Lincoln: University of Nebraska Press, 2000).

3. For an accessible, full description of the traditional *thiyóšpaye,* see Ella Deloria, *Speaking of Indians* (New York: Friendship Press, 1944; reprint, Lincoln: University of Nebraska Press, 1998).

4. A detailed history of the Sioux Nation's attempts to win back the Black Hills can be found in Edward Lazarus, *Black Hills, White Justice: The Sioux Nation Versus the United States, 1775 to the Present* (Lincoln: University of Nebraska Press, 1999).

The Use and Misuse of Lakota Religion

1. An accessible overview of modern Lakota religion can be found in Stephen E. Feraca, *Wakinyan: Lakota Religion in the Twentieth Century* (Lincoln: University of Nebraska Press, 1998). For a summary of traditional Lakota religious practices and beliefs, see James R. Walker, *Lakota Belief and Ritual,* ed. Raymond J. DeMallie and Elaine A. Jahner (Lincoln: University of Nebraska Press, 1980). An illuminating set of essays on different aspects of traditional and contemporary Lakota religion is contained in Raymond J. DeMallie and Douglas R. Parks, eds., *Sioux Indian Religion* (Norman: University of Oklahoma Press, 1987).

2. The life of Frank Fools Crow is presented in Thomas E. Mails, *Fools Crow* (New York: Doubleday, 1979; reprint, Lincoln: University of Nebraska Press, 1990).

3. *Tunkashila* (*Thųkášila*), meaning *grandfather,* is the term used in Lakota prayer to address Wakhą́ Thą́ka, the Great Spirit. Black Elk told Neihardt that he did not use the term because he "thought there was an old man sitting up there" who would hear him. He addressed Wakhą́ Thą́ka as Grandfather because it was a term of greatest respect.

4. Accounts and analyses of the Lakota sun dance can be found in Feraca, *Wakinyan;* Arthur Amiotte, "The Lakota Sun Dance: Historical and Contemporary Perspectives," in DeMallie and Parks, *Sioux Indian Religion,* pp. 75–89; and James R. Walker, "The Sun Dance and Other Ceremonies of the Oglala

Division of the Teton Dakota," *Anthropological Papers* (American Museum of Natural History) 16 (1917): 15–221.

5. *Akíchita* is an association of men who, in the old days and now, act as police, enforcing rules and customs and keeping order. See James R. Walker, *Lakota Society*, ed. Raymond J. DeMallie (Lincoln: University of Nebraska Press, 1982), pp. 28–29, 32–34.

6. For an in-depth look at the history and significance of the Lakota sweat lodge, see Raymond A. Bucko, *The Lakota Ritual of the Sweat Lodge: History and Contemporary Practice* (Lincoln: University of Nebraska Press, 1998).

7. Information about the Native American Church in South Dakota is provided by Emerson Spider Sr., "The Native American Church of Jesus Christ," in DeMallie and Parks, *Sioux Indian Religion*, pp. 189–209. See also Paul Steinmetz, "Pipe, Bible, and Peyote among the Oglala Lakota," in *Stockholm Studies in Comparative Religion*, vol. 19 (Motala: University of Sweden, 1980).

8. For a detailed look at the relationship between Catholicism and Lakota religion, see Harvey Markowitz, "The Catholic Mission and the Sioux: A Crisis in the Early Paradigm," in DeMallie and Parks, *Sioux Indian Religion*, pp. 113–137.

9. More information about Lakota holy men can be found in Thomas H. Lewis, *The Medicine Men: Oglala Sioux Ceremony and Healing* (Lincoln: University of Nebraska Press, 1990). For a recent account of a Lakota holy man's life and healing effects on others, see Gerald Mohatt and Joseph Eagle Elk, *The Price of a Gift: A Lakota Healer's Story* (Lincoln: University of Nebraska Press, 2000).

10. The traditional use and significance of the pipe is the subject of George Sword's account in Walker, *Lakota Belief and Ritual*, pp. 82–83, 87–90.

11. Raymond J. DeMallie, *The Sixth Grandfather: Black Elk's Teachings Given to John G. Neihardt* (Lincoln: University of Nebraska Press, 1984).

12. The Longest Walk, which started in the spring of 1978, was the last large-scale protest of the Red Power movement. For accounts of and reactions to the Longest Walk, see Josephy, Nagel, and Johnson, *Red Power*, pp. 53–59.

13. The term *hóchoka* here refers to the sun dance tree, but it can also be defined as "camp circle" and refer metaphorically to the people who comprise the camp.

Many Paths

1. Tobacco ties are small pieces of cloth, usually red, which are filled with tobacco or other sacred materials, bound and tied to the sun dance tree.

2. For a detailed description of the *yuwípi* ritual, see Feraca, *Wakinyan,* pp. 30–44; Thomas H. Lewis, "The Contemporary Yuwípi," in DeMallie and Parks, *Sioux Indian Religion,* pp. 173–187; and William K. Powers, *Yuwípi: Vision and Experience in Oglala Ritual* (Lincoln: University of Nebraska Press, 1982).

3. *Mitákuye oyás'į,* translated literally, means "all my relatives." It is an expression used often, and Esther explains that its meaning depends upon how it is used. For example, if used at the end of a prayer, it would mean, "this is for all my people." After a talk giving information, it might mean, "for all you people."

Lakota Legends and Stories

1. Collections of Lakota and Dakota legends and stories include James R. Walker, *Lakota Myth,* ed. Elaine A. Jahner (Lincoln: University of Nebraska Press, 1983); Zitkala-Ša, *Old Indian Legends* (Lincoln: University of Nebraska Press, 1985); Marie L. McLaughlin, *Myths and Legends of the Sioux* (Lincoln: University of Nebraska Press, 1990); and Luther Standing Bear, *Stories of the Sioux* (Lincoln: University of Nebraska Press, 1988).

Women and Men/Men and Women

1. For views on traditional Lakota customs of marriage, divorce, kinship, and gender roles, see Walker, *Lakota Society,* pp. 40–67.

2. A discussion of the role of Lakota women in modern religion is in Beatrice Medicine, "Indian Women and the Renaissance of Traditional Religion," in DeMallie and Parks, *Sioux Indian Religion,* pp. 159–171. A first-person account of a modern Lakota woman's experiences can be found in Delphine Red Shirt, *Bead on an Anthill: A Lakota Childhood* (Lincoln: University of Nebraska Press, 1997).

3. The gift of the sacred pipe is told in Neihardt, *Black Elk Speaks,* p. 3–5.

We Remember

1. Michael F. Steltenkamp, *Black Elk: Holy Man of the Oglala* (Norman: University of Oklahoma Press, 1993).

2. In about the year 1935 or 1937, as recalled by Olivia, Alex Duhamel invited Black Elk to participate in his pageant held near Rushmore, South Dakota. Black Elk and his family did so for a number of years. In a video-taped interview with Dr. Dale Stover of the University of Nebraska–Omaha, Alex Duhamel's son, Bud Duhamel, gives personal memories of the pageant and Black Elk's intentions in demonstrating and talking about Lakota cus-

toms and religious practices. The tape may be viewed at the John G. Neihardt State Historic Site in Bancroft, Nebraska. Another description of the pageant as told by Emma Amiotte, Bud Duhamel, and others is included in DeMallie, *The Sixth Grandfather.*

3. Father Placidus F. Sialm, Holy Rosary Mission.

4. Frank A. Zimmerman, S.J.

Grandfather's Healing

1. The healing of Henry Horse is also recalled by Bud Duhamel in the Duhamel-Stover videotape interview.

Index